THE 90 SECOND LAWYER™ GUIDE TO BUYING REAL ESTATE

THE 90 SECOND LAWYER™ GUIDE TO BUYING REAL ESTATE

ROBERT IRWIN
DAVID L. GANZ

JOHN WILEY & SONS, INC.
New York • Chichester • Weinheim • Brisbane • Singapore • Toronto

Copyright © 1997 by Robert Irwin and David L. Ganz, and The 90 Second Lawyer, Inc.
Published by John Wiley & Sons, Inc.

This publication is designed to provide accurate and authoritative
information in regard to the subject matter covered. It is sold
with the understanding that the publisher is not engaged in
rendering legal, accounting, or other professional services. If
legal advice or other expert assistance is required, the services
of a competent professional person should be sought.

Library of Congress Cataloging-in-Publication Data:

Irwin, Robert. 1941—
    The 90 second lawyer guide to buying real estate / by Robert
Irwin & David L. Ganz.
      p.   cm.
    Includes bibliographical references.
    ISBN 0-471-16575-1 (alk. paper)
    1. Vendors and purchasers—United States—Popular works. 2. House
buying—United States. I. Ganz, David L. II. Title.
KF665.Z9I79   1997
346.7304'363—dc20
[347.3064363]   96-38521

Printed in the United States of America

10 9 8 7 6 5 4 3 2 1

To our wives,
Rita and Kathy, with love

Preface

Owning a home, buying a home, selling a home, renting a home—more than 60 million Americans are involved in some aspect of real estate. And the vast majority of us do it on our own, without the aid of an attorney.

This doesn't mean, however, that we don't need specialized and sometimes legal advice. The field of real estate has become steadily more complex with specific requirements demanded by government at the local, state, and federal levels. Further, our litigious society has seen sellers, buyers, and landlords become increasingly susceptible to lawsuits.

What your authors discovered is that until now what has been almost entirely absent is a practical guide to protecting yourself when you're involved in a real estate transaction. So we decided to create one.

Here we break through the legal gobbledygook associated with most kinds of real estate transactions and provide the information you need to successfully complete a purchase or sale. Need to know about an "abstract of title," how big a deposit to give and who to give it to, or what the problems are when selling a home yourself? You'll find answers here. You'll also find self-help.

During nearly 20 years of practicing law and assisting hundreds of clients each year, one of the authors has found there are recurring problems that many people face. The other author has found over a comparable period that the layperson's skills are perfectly adequate for solving many of those problems. The result is a handy, portable reference source: *The 90 Second Lawyer Guide to Real Estate* is your common sense expert.

And you can get the information in no more than a "sound bite." Our goal is be concise, very. It is estimated that the average adult reads about 800 words a minute with a reasonable amount of comprehension.

Thus, each question or essay consists of about 1,200 words, more or less—about the size of a good newspaper column that is trying to cover a complicated topic with attention to the issue and its resolution.

We do not pretend that this book is a substitute for sound professional advice for the specifics of your problem, which may vary. From the facts that we have assumed in each of our examples, we also think that in many cases, you will be pleased to find that you do not need a lawyer, or other professionals, to give you assistance; with the help of this book, you will be on the right track and able to resolve your problems by yourself, quickly and profitably. In other cases, legal or accounting advice will be necessary.

Our hope is that here you will find answers to your questions concerning real estate as well as forms that will help you put these ideas into practice.

ROBERT IRWIN AND DAVID L. GANZ

Contents

FORECLOSURE

TITLE TO REAL PROPERTY

OWNERSHIP OF REAL PROPERTY

THE 90 SECOND LAWYER™ GUIDE TO BUYING REAL ESTATE

Introduction

The essence of law, as it is studied, is impossible to distill into a short book. This is especially true for real estate, which has arcane law that varies from state to state, and on which subject whole encyclopedias have been written. Indeed, the brief chapter in this book on partition of real property as a remedy for landowners who can't get along is derived from a 20,000-word essay that was originally intended as a replacement chapter in a well-known national legal real estate encyclopedia.

Before being admitted to the bar, aspirants to a law degree go to graduate school for three years and spend hundreds of hours in classroom settings studying the law in all its beauty and confusion. Many lawyers, after they are admitted, are required to take a skills-and-methods course before they are able to practice.

This book does not pretend to replace that type of training, but it is designed to get to the nub of many common problems that a typical consumer, or businessperson, is likely to run across involving real estate transactions. It offers a quick fix for a number of issues that you are likely to incur in daily life.

We've added some features to this book that we hope will make it even more user friendly.

 Every chapter contains at least one money-saving idea. If you can follow any one of them, chances are it will pay for the cost of this book, and then some. Follow all of them, and you can probably utilize the savings to purchase your next investment property.

Helpful Hint We've also shown helpful hints culled from our experience that won't save money as much as they will save you a great deal of time later on—perhaps years from now when you put your house on the market. By taking some actions now, you can minimize the work that you'll have to do later.

And we've included forms that you may want to obtain for real estate transactions.

While this book won't substitute for three years of law school education plus dozens of years of legal experience, it does offer practical information on real estate topics that you're likely to encounter.

Even if you decide that you want a lawyer to give you a hand, we think that you'll find this book saves you time and money because it will show you how to organize your complaints in a cohesive fashion—and that will allow your attorney to bill you for fewer hours of professional services.

VISIT THE 90 SECOND LAWYER ON THE INTERNET

The 90 Second Lawyer™ wants to be your source for succinct information. We recognize that we cannot anticipate all of our readers' questions in the following pages, and we plan to have additional books that form a series of questions and answers in the same format as this book.

If you have questions in the interim, you can get on-line assistance for general questions simply by posting the questions on the Internet. The 90 Second Lawyer will try to answer them for you and, if they fit our format, utilize them in our next book.

The 90 Second Lawyer welcomes your questions on real estate or other topics. We'll try and respond to them as received, and reserve the right to use them without credit, or compensation, in future volumes of *The 90 Second Lawyer* series.

You can e-mail your inquiries to:

Lawyr90Sec@aol. com

or to:

David L Ganz@aol.com

All communications become property of The 90 Second Lawyer, Inc.

Also see our internet website: http://members.aol.com/davidlganz /indexl.html

Purchasing Property

Chapter 1

Understanding the Purchase Agreement

You're about to make the most expensive purchase of a lifetime—your new home—and you're given a long and complicated document to seal the transaction. The broker who prepared it, or the lawyer involved in the drafting, expect it to be signed with a minimum of changes or difficulty, perhaps in a half hour or less.

You spend more time haggling over the price of a new car, and the extras, at the auto dealership than you do over the fine details of this transaction that costs multiples of the automobile that you drive. The automobile contract and its extras rarely require more than a page or two; the typical real estate contract is nearly 5,000 words in length.

If you have a lawyer, chances are he or she has done this a hundred times; real estate brokers do it nearly every day of the week. But this is (or is going to be) your first time, or your second time, or maybe even your third, and you're nervous about it—maybe even a little scared.

Will you be able to make the mortgage payment that's required each month? What about the real estate taxes that have to be paid twice or four times each year? And what about upkeep and maintenance on the house that you never had to worry about in an apartment or townhouse?

Many persons who have purchased homes before, as well as those who are just entering the market, wonder what it is that they are asked to sign. These agreements (sometimes covering more than 10 pages) are hardly simple and sometimes, even when written in plain language format, are not that easy to understand.

Yet, the real estate contract that forms the basis of a purchase agreement need not be very complicated, at least in theory. It actually must have only the following elements:

- A dated agreement.
- Signatures of the parties (who will sell, who will purchase).
- The amount of the purchase price to be paid.

- The amount of deposit to be made at the time the contract is signed.

- What is being purchased (the address, the block and lot, or something similar to identify it).

- The terms of the purchase (how the deposit is to be applied, the amount of cash, the amount of financing).

- A brief description of any other contingencies that the contract to purchase depends on (e.g., termite inspection).

- Other clauses needed to define the contract and protect the parties (such as "time is of the essence . . ."). Given the elementary nature of the basic purchase agreement, why the multipage contracts so commonly used today?

The answer has more to do with CYA (Cover Your "Backside") than it does with reason. Just as insurance policies often try to cover every potential loophole (you're protected against a herd of pink elephants crushing your home) so do many purchase agreements prepared by agents try to cover almost every foreseeable problem. They often have paragraphs dealing with personal property, time of possession, even delivery of keys.

Are all these "extra" clauses necessary?

Maybe. Often, however, they mostly act to protect the agent or attorney who cannot later be said to have overlooked something.

SHOULD YOU SIGN THE PREPARED
PURCHASE AGREEMENT?

That depends on who prepared it. Just who prepares the contract depends on local practice. Sometimes, real estate brokers will prepare the contract using a standard form. Other times, especially in the northeastern states, the seller's lawyer will prepare a contract of sale. In even rarer instances, the person selling or doing the purchasing will prepare the agreement.

It's always a good idea to have someone knowledgeable in real estate look over the purchase agreement before signing it. It's intended to be a legally binding contract and you need to protect yourself in it. If you've bought many properties, you may feel competent to handle this yourself. On the other hand, you may want to have an attorney check it over, just to be sure. Remember, the fees for having a real estate attorney coach you on a purchase are extraordinarily low (compared with attorney fees for other matters).

Often, the entire purchase will be handled by an attorney for $1,000, often much less if only consultation is required with no forms to be prepared. Be wary of leaning on the real estate agent for advice about the purchase contract. The vast majority of such agents are not attorneys, they are salespeople. Their knowledge of legal matters may be slim and not necessarily accurate. In some states, such as California and New York, agents are prohibited from giving legal advice.

The following sections cover some of the specific elements of the purchase agreement.

PRICE

In making the decision to purchase, perhaps the biggest factor is the price. However, once the buyer and seller agree on a figure, it is the simplest item to include in the purchase agreement. It is relatively easy to insert the legal language concerning price into the contract governing the transaction. Often, it's just a matter of filling in a dollar amount. (Be sure that the deposit given with the purchase agreement is included in the price, and not on top of the price!)

FINANCING

The next items commonly dealt with are the financing terms. Usually this involves a down payment and a new mortgage from a lender. Sometimes, on the other hand, the seller will "take back" a mortgage, helping to finance the purchase. The purchase agreement should specify where the financing is to come from (seller, institutional lender, other), the terms that the buyer wants (maximum interest rate, points, term), type of financing (fixed, adjustable, or other) and the amount. There is no specific language that must be used, except that everything should be spelled out clearly to avoid confusion. Finally, the agreement should state that if the desired financing is not obtainable, the contract is canceled.

POSSESSION

If the purchaser is to take possession before the closing, you probably need to provide who shall bear the risk of loss in the event of fire or damage to the premises. Most lawyers don't like to give

possession before closing, even if the house is vacant, because of liability issues—and the difficulty in removing the person if the deal
fails to close.

PERSONAL PROPERTY

Make a list of the personal property (not attached fixtures) that you
believe are to be included in the sale—or should be. Sellers should be
careful to exclude what they are taking (a dining room lighting fix-
ture is a common example) and what they are leaving (the three-year-
old air conditioner in the window is another example).

MORTGAGE ASSUMPTION

A buyer who wants to assume the seller's mortgage should inquire
whether the lender will allow it to be assumed.

 In some cases, mortgage assumption can save substantial mortgage recording taxes, worth thousands of dollars in savings to the consumer. This is true in states
such as New York that impose a mortgage recording tax
on "new" money lent, but not on assumed obligations.

DEPOSIT

The deposit should be kept in an interest-bearing escrow account. It
may not sound like much, but on each $10,000 of down payment, you
can earn up to $1.36 per day in interest. It typically takes 45 to 120
days to go from contract to closing. At the longer end, this means that
$164 on each $10,000 can be earned—the cost of a very nice dinner,
plus the purchase price of this book.

 Sometimes, the lawyer, broker, or seller will tell you not
to bother with the interest, because it's too hard to set
up the account. Call your local bank and ask whether a
special interest-bearing account can be set up with the
deposit money. Most will be happy to set it up as a day-of-deposit to
day-of-withdrawal savings account.

Either side can claim the interest, with justification. The seller can ask that interest follow the principal, and state that it was earned at the time the contract was entered into. The buyer can argue effectively that the deal isn't final until it closes. It's just a matter of negotiation.

FUNDING

Be sure to stipulate how funds are to be paid at closing (certified check or bank wire is best). Personal checks up to a limited amount (say $1,000) are probably reasonable. But the aim is not to get a bad check, or to have anything further to do with the other party—except on a social basis—after the closing, unless there's an ongoing economic transaction (such as a purchase money mortgage).

COMMON CLAUSES

There are some common representations that every seller is asked to make, either in the contract or purchase agreement, or prior to the sale:

- The Premises abut or have a right of access to a public road (see Chapter 29).
- Seller is the sole owner of the Premises and has the full right, power, and authority to sell, convey, and transfer the same in accordance with the terms of this contract.
- Seller is not a "foreign person," as that term is defined for purposes of the Foreign Investment in Real Property Tax Act, Internal Revenue Code (IRC Section 1445, as amended) and the regulations promulgated thereunder (collectively, FIRPTA; this has tax-withholding consequences).
- The Premises are not affected by any exemptions or abatements of taxes.
- Seller has been known by no other name for the past 10 years (if the seller has, for example, a recent marriage, it must be disclosed so that title can be checked against the spouse's name, too). Typically, the purchaser will be asked to make some representations, too.

- Purchaser has the financial wherewithal to conclude the transaction on the terms negotiated.
- Purchaser is aware of the physical condition of the premises.
- Purchaser accepts the premises, "as is" (you may want to insist that the seller warrant the condition of the premises).
- Purchaser will diligently apply for a mortgage and timely fill out all documents.
- Name of the broker that Purchaser dealt with is the only broker involved with purchaser. As you move toward this important decision for your new home, it is important to be decisive, to be honest, to be goal-oriented, and to be careful.

In the Appendix, you can examine a typical form that is used. Similar forms are available nationwide at stationery stores that carry blank legal forms. A "rider" is a supplement that is used by lawyers to augment the printed form.

Chapter 2

How Can I Effectively
Use Contingency Clauses?

You've read the form contract, and understand it, and are ready to buy a new home or sell your existing residence. But what do you do if you can't pay all cash for the home from your own funds (nearly all buyers can't)? What if the prospective purchaser will only make a purchase if you fix the broken fence at the rear of your lot? These and other concerns are dealt with in the contract by using contingency clauses.

Contingency clauses go hand-in-hand with real estate sales contracts—there are usually several in every contract. They are often a means by which buyers and sellers protect themselves. Contingency clauses are special terms and conditions that are part of an "if . . . then" logic. For example, most real estate contracts provide that *if* the buyer can't get a mortgage, *then* the contract is canceled.

This is an understandable contingency, since most individuals require outside financing to complete the transaction. It is also typical for many contracts to provide that *if* the buyer secures and approves a home inspection report, *then* the deal may go forward. Many sellers protect themselves with an added contingency clause which may say, *if* the buyer does not approve the report within seven days, *then* seller is under no further obligation to sell property to buyer. Or, *if* repairs found in the engineering report exceed $1,000, *then* seller has the option of canceling the contract in lieu of completing them, or the buyer can decide to take the premises, "as is."

CONTINGENCIES FOR EVERYONE AND EVERYTHING

Contingencies can't be characterized as being used exclusively by sellers or exclusively by buyers. Both sides want to have certain elements included in the contract that give them rights, to the exclusion of the other side. Typically, the contingencies deal with impediments that may be anticipated, or those that are feared. Working out a clear understanding in advance makes for a viable contract. Here are some of the most common contingencies found in a real estate contract to purchase or sell property:

- Mortgage contingency clause.
- Mortgage rate.
- Mortgage length and duration (term).
- Seller financing (purchase money mortgage).
- Limitation on amount of required repairs.
- Engineering report.
- For both condominiums and cooperative apartments, the approval of the Board of Directors of the Association.
- For commercial property, that the certificate of occupancy will permit a lawful use contemplated by the prospective purchaser.
- For new construction, that a building permit can (or will) be issued.
- For completed new construction, that the issuance of certificate of occupancy or certificate of completion will not be withheld.
- Occupancy, that it be given by a certain date.

CREATING A CONTINGENCY CLAUSE

It is important to carefully think through contingency clauses before putting them into contracts. The obvious reason is that if the "if . . . then" is not fulfilled, the typical consequence is that the contract is voided, and the parties are free to go about their business as if the contract didn't exist. In other words, the contingency clause is a contract burner. Usually, this is not desirable from a seller's standpoint, and equally, most times the buyer doesn't want to allow the seller to put the property back on the market and sell it at a higher price to somebody else. Here are some common sense concerns when creating the contingency clause:

Helpful Hint When you are negotiating for a contingency clause, look at your request from the other side's perspective. The more reasonable that you are willing to make the request, the more likely that the contingency will be granted.

Helpful Hint When it comes time to negotiate a mortgage contingency clause, some buyers who really want the house and do not want to let it get away, consider not putting in any mortgage contingency clause. In other words, they'll buy the house and, as far as the seller is concerned, pay cash! It's a terrific negotiating tool, but *don't* do this unless you're fully assured of getting the money from a lender. You are risking not only your deposit, but your legal well-being as well.

Sometimes, a contingency clause that you ask for will be a deal breaker. You may ask for something that seems very reasonable to you—and maybe even to the real estate broker, or even a lawyer—but simply isn't to the other side. Recently, one of the authors became acquainted with a client who wanted to purchase a house that was still being renovated. The seller didn't mind having an engineering report, but balked because of time and cost at supplying a certificate of occupancy or sign-off on the electrical work and plumbing, even though the work was being done by licensed professionals. The proposal was that the contract be made contingent on receipt by the purchasers of such approvals. The seller refused to agree to the contingency.

As a result, the buyer faced a choice of whether or not to sign a contract that guaranteed that the electric and plumbing would be in good working order, or one that included a clause stating that the premises had been officially inspected, and given a municipal sign-off. The buyer really wanted the house and made a business decision—not a legal determination—to forgo the municipal approval. The stronger contingency was eliminated in favor of the weaker one.

A contingency is typically written right into the sales agreement. It can be in plain English and may say something such as, "Purchase of property is contingent on buyer securing and approving a home inspection report within 7 days. Approval to be in the form of a written statement of approval presented to seller. If approval is not presented to the seller within the time allotted, contract is automatically canceled." Such a contingency should always have a finish to the thought, What if there isn't approval? Is the contract automatically canceled, or can the purchaser still go ahead? That's a matter of negotiation.

CONTINGENCIES TO WATCH FOR

Perhaps the most technical contingencies occur in the boilerplate of most contracts of sale requiring the seller to tender marketable title. Sometimes, this will be changed to insurable title—a key distinction. Watch out for the contract that gives the seller a right to cancel if marketable or insurable title cannot be produced. It's a sure sign that the seller anticipates difficulties that could jeopardize the closing:

- It's not at all unusual for a seller to have liens on the property— especially mortgages—that would be an impediment on the title, which should otherwise be free and clear. Usually, the contract simply provides that closing proceeds can be used to satisfy the lien.

- Repairs to the premises are an often overlooked clause. It's fair to ask for a seller to keep the premises in good repair. The sale is usually subject to "reasonable wear and tear" from the signing of the contract until the closing—which can be four or five months later.

 Be certain to make it clear that anything beyond reasonable wear and tear is the seller's responsibility. That way, if the seller throws a farewell party for the neighborhood that gets out of hand, it's on his bill, not yours.

Be certain that if there is a contingency, you understand what it is, and how it is to be dealt with. Also assure yourself that the contingency is spelled out clearly and succinctly, so that you understand your rights and liabilities.

 Sometimes, it pays to think ahead as to what may be required when you, the new buyer, want to resell. If your community normally requires a certificate of completion for all new additions to a house, if you don't insist on it with a contingency at the time that you make the purchase, you might have to dig into your pocket and pay a contractor or professional to obtain that certificate at the time that you resell (or suffer a financial consequence you hadn't intended).

Chapter 3

Do I Need a Lawyer
When I Buy a Home?

No. But doing without a lawyer may not necessarily be the wisest course of action. Simply put, it may be risky to be unrepresented, although it is done all the time in states such as California and Florida. Typically in such states, the title insurance company and the real estate agents handle much of the work that an attorney does in other parts of the country, such as New York. On the other hand, some states, such as New York, won't allow title companies to work with nonlawyers. Other states, such as New Jersey, have only recently changed to permit it.

It is probably more important to have title examination undertaken than it is to have representation in making the purchase, assuming that you can read a contract and understand it. But having a lawyer can be useful if there is negotiating to do that you're not comfortable handling yourself—or if you need someone to play the "bad guy" to your "good guy" routine.

The Appendix to this book contains several standard forms that have been successfully used in buying and selling real estate. They have few surprises and work very well. If the transaction isn't all that complex, you may very well be able to do it without hiring a lawyer, though that will leave one of the authors very unhappy.

WHAT A LAWYER COSTS

Cost is the most compelling reason individuals avoid using a lawyer as part of the real estate transaction. In the "good old days" before the Supreme Court of the United States eliminated the practice, bar associations used to publish a list of suggested fees that should be charged for various transactions. On most residential real property transactions, the fee recommended for counsel was 1 percent. Of course, this was more than 30 years ago, but the typical $500 fee for closing costs on a residential property, then, would be the approximate equivalent of $5,000 in today's dollars—a sum that only the most difficult or time consuming of transactions might warrant. However, more than likely, today, on a residential property purchase, fees charged by counsel for an uncomplicated transaction will resemble the unadjusted 1967 fee schedule approved by the Bar Association—no inflation taken into account.

That's right: For the most important economic transaction that you are likely to enter into in your lifetime, a legal fee of between $500 and $1,000 is what you might expect to pay. In other words, it's the cheapest legal advice you're ever likely to get. (To beat that speeding ticket or DUI charge with competent legal counsel will likely cost a lot more.)

THE LEGAL FORMS

One of the most important functions a lawyer can perform in a purchase is to examine and/or prepare the documents, including the purchase agreement. Many years ago, when New York title companies routinely provided complimentary contracts of sale (purchase agreements), many material terms were omitted. One of them always related to the condition of the appliances in the house at the time of closing, and the condition or state of the roof.

As soon as an attorney came on board, virtually every time he would add a rider that the appliances would be in good working order at the time of closing, and the roof would be free of leaks. Eventually, a joint committee of the Bar Association and the Real Estate Board, amended the standard contract—and included this as well as many other clauses. The residential contract of sale found in the Appendix is one such form. Even with that, riders are still used.

An experienced attorney knows what to look for in these contracts, and what to have omitted. You, of course, don't; so feel free to read it. Most of the time, things make sense. But not always. You may come across an arcane provision that makes no sense to you, yet is simply not negotiable. The reason for this is also clear: Law likes predictability, and each of the printed clauses in the contract is designed to obtain a predictable result.

Again, it is wisest to have an attorney whom you can ask. Real estate agents may also be able to provide answers; however, in some states they are specifically prohibited from giving "legal advice."

WHAT TO DO IF YOU DON'T USE A LAWYER

If you do not want a lawyer, it is probably wise to insist that any forms used for the purchase contract or any riders, should be approved by either the local real estate board or one of the local Bar Associations. The reason is that these preprinted forms inevitably reflect local practice and are typically what the representative of your choice would probably be negotiating for anyway. Further, in a typical residential transaction involving the purchase of a home with a mortgage or deed of trust, a title company that routinely clears titles, prepares deeds, and so forth can often handle the paperwork because it is a routine aspect of the real estate transaction.

When your own lawyer reads a preprinted real estate contract, it doesn't take long because it's the same in virtually every transaction. The differences are found in any riders. That's why its relatively easy (and not a lot of time) to have a lawyer read most real estate documents.

 Here, then, is the trade-off: time or money. That's the choice that you have to make. It may make sense to hire someone; or, to keep costs down, there are some aspects that you may be able to do yourself.

TASKS THAT LAWYERS, OR YOU, NEED TO PERFORM

About half a day will be devoted to the contract signing, and another half day for the closing. The rest of the time is following up with the mortgage company, making sure that the surveyor listed the property and ascertaining whether or not the exterminator has found vermin or other insects, and a whole host of other items, including ordering, and then reading, the title report. Then, the lawyer must clear any title defects or obtain affirmative insurance against some of them. Virtually every residence does have some title defects.

Most of them, however, are not serious. For example, someone with a name similar to yours may have once gotten a parking ticket from a municipal authority. Some people might consider this as a lien or potential lien on the property, but the title company typically calls this to your attention. The cure for this is an affidavit indicating that you are not the person against whom the judgment has been entered. It could be complicated if it turns out that you are the person with the parking violation, now reduced to a judgment. Typically, the bank is going to require that you satisfy this prior to the closing, and you may have to do this by appearing in court or other municipal office, and then payable, in full, the amount of the judgment together with interest that has accrued, and certain other statutory costs. All of this can be time consuming. But, you can do it yourself (with aid from the title insurance company and/or the agent), or have an attorney do it. You may also find that the legal description by the surveyor in metes and bounds does not match the survey, or the street report accompanying the title report may show that the parcel you purchased is landlocked without access to the nearest legally opened street. All of these problems often can be solved fairly easily at least after negotiation or discussion with the title company.

WHAT TO LOOK FOR

If you do not use an attorney, here is a list of key items that you will want to make sure are included in your title report, and are without defects:

- *Survey.* The survey of the land is a guarantee to the title company, and guarantee to you. In some locations, a reading survey is utilized; in others, a survey inspection can be used together with an affidavit with no change, signed by the current owner. Regardless, you want this read into your title report.
- *Survey Readings.* The survey is read and described in a brief paragraph.
- *Survey Inspection.* If the survey is more than a year old, you want to be certain that there have been no material changes since it was made.
- *Tax Search.* This shows whether the taxes on the premises have been paid, and what is presently "open" that needs to be paid in order to stay free and clear of any tax liens.
- *Tax Description.* This assures that the taxes that have been searched cover the correct lot and block, and also gives a general legal description of the premises.
- *Certificate of Occupancy.* This describes what the residence may be legally used for, the number of rooms, its height, and anything

that is particularly unusual about the premises, such as a separate garage, built-in garage, ground pool, and so forth.

- *Street Report.* This ascertains whether or not the street is legally opened with full risks, and shows both streets on which the premises are located, and one or more of the nearest residential streets to it. Without this, you have land that you may not be able to legally get to.

- *Building Department Violations.* Searches for violations that are of record.

- *Fire Department Violations.* Searches for fire department violations of record.

- *Emergency Repairs.* In some jurisdictions, the municipality has the right to make emergency repairs on the premises. This checks for liens that may exist.

- *Street Widening.* In some municipalities, the government has the right to take property without additional compensation) for pre-existing proposed roadways if they are widened. The reason for this is that compensation was paid in the first place at the time that the road was laid out. In New York City, for example, § 35 of the City Charter provides for this. The title company can give you affirmative insurance, if necessary, against some widening.

- *Existence of Liens.* A search of lower and upper courts (which form liens) for judgments; a search of the bankruptcy court.

TIPS FOR DOING IT YOURSELF

If you do decide to purchase a house without using a lawyer, here are some handy tips that ought to be among your chief concerns, and some resolutions to thorny problems. Some are real money-savers for you.

- Choose your title company carefully. Look for a company that specializes in service. Rates probably won't be very different; service is, however.

- Insist on getting closing cost estimates up front—especially if making the purchase is going to strain your finances. Ask the title company how long it will take from contract signing to closing and consider whether that accommodates your financial and other needs.

See if the title company will let you use an older survey and inspect the property for changes instead of using a new survey. If it is less than 10 years old, odds are they'll allow it and you'll save a lot of money.

 Find out who is responsible for the real property transfer tax customarily in your jurisdiction, and then try to make sure it's not you. If it is, try to negotiate it with the seller or seller's attorney. In some jurisdictions, there is a 2 percent tax that the seller is required to pay, but it is customarily split between buyer and seller. If you're the seller, consider negotiating on that point. If you're the buyer, you can always insist that the law be followed.

If you do decide that you want a lawyer to help with your house closing, ask for an up-front estimate of the cost—and consider asking for a fixed fee representation. For an uncomplicated residential real estate transaction, expect that it will take your lawyer 10 to 12 hours of time to get the work done. It could be more, or less. Be prepared to pay for that time. It is no longer uncommon for lawyers to advertise their fees for handling real estate transactions.

 The local pennysaver in your community may well have ads from lawyers who hope for volume, and offer a relatively low price. They will use many forms similar to the ones in this book, and save time in drafting.

If service is your priority, however, ask the lawyer what kind of service you'll get—and then ask yourself if you'll be happy with it.

Chapter 4

How Should I Handle the Deposit?

In a typical real estate transaction, whether it involves buying, leasing or renting, a deposit, also called "earnest money" or "good faith money" is commonly used. The purpose of these funds is to benefit both buyer and seller. From the buyer's standpoint, it locks the seller into the deal by creating an enforceable contract; from the seller's standpoint, the buyer is locked in, too, since failure to go forward could result in a forfeiture of the deposit.

HOW MUCH?

There is no legally required amount. It can be one dollar or a hundred thousand dollars. The amount, however, should be large enough to allay the seller's fear that the buyer will back out, yet small enough not to worry the buyers that a lifetime's worth of savings could be lost if for some unforeseen reason they must back out of the deal. Some concerns about the amount are these: Basically, the higher the selling price, the fewer the amount of dollars as a percentage amount of that sales price, that the purchaser wants to have at risk. Further, a lower sum is warranted where the earnest money is not placed in an interest-bearing account, or where the purchase price is so substantial that the loss or forfeiture would probably be subjected to penalty, and hence voided by the court.

Typically, the contractual arrangements will provide that the seller may retain the earnest money if the buyer fails to close the contract provided. Unless "time is of the essence" (which is a clause included in most real estate contracts), this typically does not mean on the precise time specified on the contract, but rather "on or about" a specific closing date.

WHO GETS THE DEPOSIT?

- It is important to consider who should hold the deposit. In theory, since the contract is with the sellers, the funds are theirs to hold. However, this usually provokes (justified) worry and concern on the part of the buyer. If the deal does not go through due to no fault of the buyers, will the sellers have the money on hand to return, or will they have spent it?

- If a real estate broker is involved, should he or she hold the deposit? Brokers are required to have trust accounts into which they place deposits. But most refuse to do so. They are afraid that if the deal goes sour, they will be caught in the middle with both buyers and sellers demanding the money. (The biggest reason for suspension or revocation of real estate licenses in most states is the improper use of money from the real estate agent's trust funds.)

- Here is a big surprise: Many lawyers feel the same way. Some always prefer that another responsible party hold the funds.

- The result is that the funds are usually deposited to escrow, where they remain until *both* parties agree they can be properly disposed of. Regardless of who holds the deposit, however, it is essential that the person be required to do so in trust, and in an escrow arrangement.

INTEREST ON THE DEPOSIT

If the funds are held in escrow, ask at the time that the contract is entered into whether or not an interest-bearing account is a possibility. If it is, insist that the funds bear interest and then negotiate who the beneficiary of the interest will be.

Suppose that you were going to buy a house for $250,000, you have put up a $20,000 deposit, and you estimate that it will take 120 days from the time that the contract is entered into, until the transaction is closed. At 5 percent, this could amount to the loss of over $400 or more in interest. You should bargain for the use of that money—or its interest.

 You could suggest to the seller that you will reduce your deposit to $10,000 instead of $20,000. On each $5,000 that you reduce the deposit, figure that your savings will be about $1 per day. Over 120 days, your savings will be substantial. No, it's not enough to buy a new car, but it's certainly a nice dinner, or two, for you and your spouse.

HINTS ON HANDLING DEPOSITS

• Never authorize the release of your deposit prior to the closing.
  It is a trust fund as long as it is treated as such. Remember, if it
  is removed from that category, it becomes part of the general assets of the seller, and if the seller were to file for bankruptcy, or
  a creditor starts to attack the money, you could wind up in an
  expensive lawsuit trying to resolve it.

• Always specify that the deposit is to become part of the down
  payment (or be returned to you). Otherwise, the seller could demand both the deposit and a down payment.

GETTING THE DEPOSIT BACK

It can be simple or very difficult. Some brokers now ask that both
parties sign a liquidated damages agreement as part of the sales
agreement. In the event the deal doesn't go through, the buyer agrees
to give up the deposit and the seller agrees not to sue for "specific
performance." If you are asked to sign such an agreement, consult
with an attorney who is cognizant of all the conditions of the sale. It
may not be in your best interest to sign. If there is no such agreement, then typically the money remains in escrow until *both* parties
agree to its dispersal.

The seller may be more inclined to agree if a new buyer, ready,
willing, and able to purchase, is found. The old buyer's deposit on the
old deal could tie up the new deal. A buyer threatening to take the
seller to court can also be a motivating factor. (A lawyer's letter can
be helpful, here). A seller, on the other hand, can claim that a buyer
is bound by the sales agreement and barring an "escape clause" (see
Chapter 5), loses the deposit.

There was a time when it was predictable that in the event of a
buyer's breach, the seller could retain liquidated damages and resell
the property. That state of the law developed when houses sold for an
average of $20,000, and the down payment was $2,000 or so. When
houses began moving into six-figure selling prices, and upward, some
courts began to construe loss of a 10 percent down payment as a
penalty, or forfeiture, which the law does not prefer. Some courts now
infer a term of "up to" the full amount of the down payment being
payable from the set-aside funds (based on actual losses).

Sellers should be aware, however, that even today many purchase contracts are so loosely written that enforcement is not automatic by the courts. In the end, getting mutual agreement for both parties can be more a matter of getting half a loaf than risking loss of the entire loaf.

GIFTING THE DEPOSIT

If you're a first-time home buyer, and the deposit (later to be used as part of the down payment) is coming from relatives as a gift, or a bridge loan, make sure they realize that the mortgage company will probably require them to sign a "gift" letter indicating that they have given you the down payment, or a portion of it, as a gift and that they have no right to reclaim it.

Such gifts are being used with greater frequency to help first-time home buyers get over the hump of coming up with an increasingly high down payment—and also of assuring that they have the resources to complete the transaction.

- Some lenders of late have not been satisfied with a gift letter but have insisted that the person making the gift sign on as a mortgagor—in effect, a cosigner. This arrangement is fraught with problems, and you should consider seeking a different and more reasonable lender if such a demand is made.

 If a gift exceeds $10,000 from one person to another, a federal gift tax return is required. To save that tax, if parents are making a gift to a child, both parents can be the donor (allowing $20,000 to be gifted), and if the child is married, a like sum can be given to the spouse (thus allowing $40,000 to be gifted at any one time without a gift tax obligation).

Chapter 5

How Do I Back Out of a Deal Gracefully?

You have made the deal of a lifetime to buy your dream house. Only now, you discover that you have been transferred out of state and can't live there. Or, your spouse simply can't bear to move on such short notice or can't stand the property. Or, the cash you thought was coming from Uncle Fred, isn't. What do you do, and more importantly, what *don't* you do to get out of the deal?

VERBAL OR WRITTEN?

First, is it simply a handshake or a written contract? As Samuel Goldwyn once put it, "A verbal contract isn't worth the paper it's printed on." Succinctly explained, for a real estate contract to be enforceable, it must be:

- In writing.
- Dated.
- Signed by the party to be charged.
- All of the material terms must be contained within the four corners of the document.

If it's only a verbal agreement, you're in luck. Bite the bullet, and tell the real estate agent that you are simply not going to proceed with the purchase. This is true whether you are the buyer or the seller. Usually, that will end any liability that you may have because of the typical requirement that the real estate contract be in writing to satisfy the statute of frauds.

Even if you are a seller given deposit money for a "binder," you probably won't incur any legal liability: Most real estate "binders" really aren't contracts in and of themselves; rather they are an agreement to make an agreement, which is generally not enforceable.

GETTING OUT OF A WRITTEN SALES AGREEMENT

If you have signed a written contract, don't despair, either. Although they are designed to be ironclad, there are usually some real estate angles that a prudent person can pursue in an effort to break the contract. Here are some to consider:

- At a minimum, for many years, it was fairly common advice to a potentially breaching seller that the high cost of litigation works in their favor. This means that it was unlikely that buyer would sue for specific performance—unless the buyer was a professional purchaser. That's probably still reasonable advice, but if the stakes are high enough, a suit for specific performance on a properly drawn real estate contract will almost always result in a purchaser's verdict (see *Bregman v. Meehan* 125 Misc. 2d 332, 479 N.Y.S.2d 422 (Sup. Ct. Nassau Co. NY, 1984)).

- In the past, one school of thought has suggested that a breaching seller could rely on federal bankruptcy law to also avoid the obligation of selling. It calls for the seller to file for Chapter 11 or Chapter 13 bankruptcy (reorganization), and then to reject the executory contract. It sounds good in theory, and has worked in some instances, but some sources have viewed this as a little more than sophistry and not permitted (see *In re Meehan,* 59 B.R. 380 (E.D.N.Y. 1986)).

- If you have just signed the contract, and your state has a "attorney review," you can have your lawyer write a formal letter canceling the agreement. (The lawyer reviewed it and found it wanting.) Just be sure that you do this within the statutory time frame, or you will find yourself in the unenviable position of trying to explain why the agreement should be canceled, rather than being able to do it as a right.

- If you are a seller, and in your jurisdiction the lawyer customarily draws the contract of purchase and sale, if the agreement has not yet been forwarded to, or returned from the buyer, or prospective buyer, you can have your counsel fax or otherwise notify the borrower's attorney that the offer is withdrawn, and that there is no longer authority to sign the agreement. Again, as is true in all cases, timing is everything for this to work.

- If you are prepared to put your deposit at risk, the estoppel letter canceling the contract and requesting the deposit back is likely to result in a contract being canceled. The issue then, is whether some portion of the deposit will be refunded, or if the seller will look at it as a windfall or bonus. Some states, increasingly, have moved toward not allowing 10 percent of the purchase price to constitute liquidated damages. The prices of houses are now simply too high. Instead, they allow the deposit to be used to offset provable loss, with the difference being refunded to the perspective purchaser who has now backed out of the deal.

- Sometimes, a buyer will use the mortgage contingency clause found in nearly all sales agreements to get out of the deal. Here the buyer simply does not cooperate with the mortgage lender, and hence is turned down for the financing. The theory goes, no financing, no deal. If you are turned down on the financing for legitimate reasons, there is nothing the matter with this. It is seemingly a great way to void a contract.

- However, smart sellers, or their lawyers, usually can smell out a recalcitrant borrower very quickly and can discover if you were truly turned down or just failed to cooperate. In the latter case, the net result is that not only might you wind up forfeiting your deposit, but you will probably be accused of bad faith, as well.

- Then there is the "poison bullet" approach. If you are strapped for cash, and it is your first house, almost inevitably the lender will ask whether or not you are receiving assistance from a family member to complete the transaction. Probably more than two-thirds of first home buyers in fact do this. Here, a buyer can use this to advantage: Instead of signing a "gift" letter, a family member can instead sign a letter stating that the buyer had to sign an "IOU" to borrow the money from them—and that it is payable in a relatively short period of time.

 If the loan repayment schedule is actually true, it is better than you imagine. It probably will kill the mortgage opportunity because lenders normally won't allow such borrowing of a down payment. And you're out on the financing contingency, cost-free. (Note: This probably won't work for FHA loans where new rules allow borrowing from family members for the down payment.)

In *Hamlet,* Shakespeare has Polonius say, "To thine own self be true!" When it comes to backing out of a deal, gracefully or not, that motto should set the standard for your actions.

Chapter 6

Do I Need a Home Inspection?

At least 5,000 separate components go into every home. With so many, it's very likely that some may be defective, even in a brand-new dwelling. In some cases, these defects simply do not matter. Who cares, really, if the kitchen sink does not have a drain cover. You can pick one up at the hardware store for under $2.00. This isn't the type of problem to lose sleep over. On the other hand, there are many other components whose workings, and condition, are far more serious. If the roof is not free of leaks, it could cost 5 percent of the purchase price, or more, to put a new one on.

If the plumbing does not work, or the heating is defective, thousands of dollars could easily be spent to rectify the situation. Even a "handyman's special" or "Fixer-Upper" generally is not sold totally "as is," for there may be certain safety hazards that the seller will be willing to correct just to avoid liability, or there may be defects that the lender will insist be corrected before funding the mortgage. The real question becomes, what are those defects? What is wrong with the home?

GETTING THE INSPECTION

Unless you're very knowledgeable about property and can conduct an inspection on your own, you're going to want to hire a competent person to do it for you. You're going to want to get a professional's opinion as to the true condition of the property. These days, very frequently buyers write into the sales agreement a demand for an inspection and make the purchase of the home contingent on their approval of the inspection. In other words, if you as the buyer don't approve the inspection, you aren't required to complete the purchase and you get your deposit back.

 Many times, sellers—for obvious reasons—won't want to let you make the deal contingent on the inspection. Why, they may argue, should they take the house off the market while you can get out of the deal simply by disapproving of a report? One solution is to limit the inspection contingency by time. Give yourself, the buyer, one week to approve the report. If you haven't gotten an inspection and approved it within a week, the seller is no longer committed. That's reasonable for both parties.

The inspection itself is usually ordered by the buyer (although sellers can handle this just as well) usually with the help of the agent and/or the lawyer, if one is involved in the transaction. Usually, it is done by a licensed contractor, or someone skilled at an examination that may include peering under floorings, checking electrical wirings, and spending part of the day looking over your new prospective home, top to bottom.

FINDING AN INSPECTOR

- Be aware that in most states inspectors are not yet licensed. Anyone, including the authors and you, the reader, can hang out a shingle and call himself or herself an "inspector." You must check out credentials carefully.
- Does the inspector belong to a professional organization? There are many state organizations and nationally there are ASHI (American Association of Home Inspectors) and NAHI (National Association of Home Inspectors).
- Will the inspector give you a written report? Will it be detailed?
- Will the inspector give you a warranty, that is will he or she stand by the conclusions stated in the report? Or will they fill their agreement with disclaimers, exclusions, and exceptions so that ultimately it guarantees nothing?
- Will the inspector provide a list of previous clients whom you can call for recommendations? If not, why not?
- Does the inspector have a background in the field? Is he or she an engineer, former building department inspector, or other person familiar with construction, particularly remodeling? (A contractor of new buildings may not really know much about the problems of older ones.)

THE INSPECTION REPORT

Your job is to review the defects that are noted and decide whether it is worthwhile to proceed with the transaction. Significantly, the timing of the report—and what the underlying contract provides (if it has been perfected at this point in time)—and the scope of its contents will define what happens next. In some states, it is customary to undertake the inspection before you even go to contract. In that way, the defects become a negotiating point. In other states, the contract may typically provide that an inspection should be made within 10 or 15 days, and then usually provides a write-cancellation based on the results. (A buyer who doesn't like the result may make a written cancellation without further penalty.)

 If you are a seller and don't want to make many repairs (or any), it is wise to limit the dollar value of any repairs that might be contemplated. Typically, a clause to this effect might read: If the repairs suggested by the building inspection report aggregate more than $500, seller shall have the right to cancel the contract which shall be of no further force or effect. Sometimes, the seller has to pay the cost of the report if the sale is canceled. The cost itself will vary, but typically it runs between $250 and $300. If specialized reports are required, such as a structural analysis, soil engineering, and so on, the cost can escalate to as much as $1,500 or more.

DISCLOSURES

Increasingly, states are requiring sellers to provide buyers with a disclosure report revealing any defects that are in the property. In New York, a recent appellate court case held a seller (and the broker) liable because they failed to disclose the local legend, which had been written up in *The Reader's Digest*,* that the subject property was haunted by a poltergeist. If you're a seller, you should be careful to include everything possible on this report.

---

*Every book on law should have a footnote, since lawyers use them all the time in their writing. It occurs to us that this type of disclosure, while it might not stand a ghost of a chance in other states, should be used about any condition known to the seller that might diminish the value (or resale potential) of the property. The case, by the way, is *Stambovsky v. Ackley*, 169 A.D.2d 254, 572 N.Y.S.2d 672 (Appellate Division, 1st Dep't [N.Y.] 1991). The complete court decision can also be found at our website, http://members.pdl.com/davidlganz/index2.html.

Once the buyer accepts it, it can be used as a defense if the buyer later comes back and demands something be repaired or replaced. In other words, you already reported it as defective and the buyer bought the property with that knowledge. Buyers should check disclosures carefully and may want to demand that significant problems be corrected prior to sale. However, not everything may be on a disclosure statement. The seller may simply not know about a crack in the foundation or a flaw in the furnace (or may conveniently have forgotten to note it). Hence, even with a disclosure report, you still need a home inspection.

WHAT SHOULD BE CHECKED

Here's a checklist of some of the items that a home inspection ought to consider. Some are obvious and are unlikely to be omitted. Others are less obvious, and potentially the cause of trouble later if you don't check it out before contract, or sale:

- Is the roof free of leaks?
- Do the heating and air conditioning units work?
- If window air conditioners, or through-the-wall air conditioners are included in the sale, is there sufficient power for them to all run, at the same time, on the existing circuitry?
- Are there storm windows in good repair on all of the window openings?
- Are there screens in good repair for windows that open?
- Does the outside hose connection work; are the automatic sprinklers in good repair?
- If there's an attic fan, does it work, and do any associated devices properly work?
- Do all of the toilets properly flush and fill, and then turn off, or is there a slow leak?
- If there's a fireplace, is it properly vented?
- Do the appliances included in the sale all work; are all switches functional; do they drain properly if water is involved?
- Are the sidewalk and driveway in good repair, or will they require high-cost maintenance in the near future?
- Has fresh paint been applied to hide a multitude of sins?

Ask the building inspector to check out the plumbing for leaks. The easiest way to do this: keep the house perfectly still without using the bathrooms or any other plumbing fixtures for about 15 minutes. Then check the water meter; it shouldn't be functioning at all. If it is, you have a slow leak—that could add up to big fees on the water.

 If the house was recently purchased and is now being resold, ask for the name of the engineer who did the previous inspection, and inquire if that inspector will cut the fee based on updating the prior report.

TERMITES

Besides the usual building inspection, a termite inspection is also warranted in some areas of the country. If there's a problem, the seller usually has the responsibility to pay for professional treatment to wipe out the insects—but not the damage that they've already done—or to cancel the contract.

 Get the name of the exterminator who does the termite work; you may be able to get a discount on quarterly extermination of pests based on the initial work on the termites—if you ask for it.

CAN YOU DO THE INSPECTION YOURSELF?

Yes, indeed, if you are the least bit handy. One of your authors has even published a book describing how to do it (*Home Inspection Troubleshooter,* Robert Irwin, Dearborn, 1995). If you're wise, however, you'll both hire an inspector and go along on the inspection. Far more is revealed that way than by reading a report prepared later on.

Selling Property

Chapter 7

What Should I Look for in a Listing Agreement?

When you hire an agent to sell your house (almost 90 percent of all properties are sold this way), you will be asked to sign a listing agreement. This is the contract that specifies what the agent is to do for you and in return, how you are to pay the agent for those services. Read the listing agreement carefully. It is designed to be a binding agreement and may lock you into all sorts of commitments that you may, or may not, want.

TYPES OF LISTING AGREEMENTS

It comes as a surprise to many people that there are many different types of listings. Don't automatically assume that the type your agent wants you to sign is the only one:

- *Open Listing.* This means that you'll agree to pay a commission to any agent who brings you a qualified buyer. But, you won't list exclusively with any one agent. Agents won't usually work under this type of listing because there's no guarantee they'll get paid, even after spending time and money promoting your property.
- *Exclusive Agency.* Here you'll agree to tie up your property with only one agent. You'll pay a commission to that agent, even if another agent has the buyer. (Your agent will typically cooperate or "co-broker" with other agents.) However, if you find a buyer on your own, you don't owe a commission. Agents don't like these, either, because of the chance that you'll get together with a buyer the agent found, say it's your buyer, and try to avoid the commission. Inevitably, this results in a lawsuit.
- *Exclusive Right-to-Sell.* You agree to pay an agent the commission no matter who finds the buyer, even if you're the one who finds him. Obviously, agents like this best because you're completely committed. This is the most commonly used listing and if

you want an agent to spend time and money promoting your property, you'll probably want to sign it.

- *Net Listing.* Watch out for this one! Here you set a price and the agent gets anything over that amount. The problem is that there's too much incentive for an unscrupulous agent to get you to set a very low price, then sell for much more, pocketing the difference. If you do use a net listing, be sure you specify that you will be made aware of the exact amount of the true sales price and that you have the right to refuse to sell if you think the amount the agent is receiving is too high.

▶ In some states, such as New York, a net listing agreement is illegal, and a broker who enters into one not only can lose his or her license, but also can forfeit the commission it is intended to generate.

All listing agreements are filled with boilerplate. However, what's said in the boilerplate, as well as what's written in by hand can be very important. Here are some areas to watch out for:

- *Term.* The listing should have a specific start date and end date. In other words, it should be for an exact term. Typically listings are for three months or longer. If an agent wants a very long listing, it's usually because market conditions are bad. Listings of over three months are probably unwarranted in most circumstances. Remember, you're locked in during the term. If the agent doesn't perform as you want, there's little you can do (see also Chapter 8).

- *Due Date for Commission Payment.* The listing should also stipulate when payment of the commission is due. In theory, the commission is due when the agent procures a buyer who is ready, willing, and able to purchase. However, as a practical matter, the commission should not be payable until the close of escrow, when your property actually sells.

- *Responsibilities of Agent.* The listing should specify what the agent will do for you. Normally this is couched in vague language such as the agent agrees to "diligently use professional efforts to procure a qualified buyer." You may want to add that the agent will advertise your property in a local newspaper, hold at least two open houses, and so on. Ultimately, however, you can't control how the agent finds a buyer. You can only hope for the best.

- *Price.* The listing should specify exactly the price your are asking. This is critical in today's market. Ask too much and buyers won't even bother to stop by. Ask too little and you lose money. To help you decide you should ask the agent for a printout of all comparable properties sold in the past year in your area.

- *Terms.* Examples are "all cash," "20 percent down," or "seller will hold 10 percent second mortgage." If you aren't specific, an agent could claim the commission by producing a buyer who is willing to pay the price, but offers terms you don't like.

- *Deposit.* You should specify the minimum deposit you'll allow the agent to accept from a buyer. You can write in any amount, but usually it's 1 to 10 percent of the sales price. Generally, you want a deposit big enough to ensure that the buyer is serious about purchasing your property. Keep in mind that agents will likely bring you every offer made regardless of the amount of the deposit. It's important to understand that there is no rule of thumb here. You must use your own judgment.

- *Sign and Keybox.* The agreement usually specifies that you allow the agent to put a sign and a locked keybox on your property. The sign is one of the best advertisements, but if you don't want one, you should let the agent know. Similarly, a keybox lets agents show your property when you're not home—essential because buyers won't wait at your convenience. However, if you do allow a keybox, just to be safe, remove all your valuables during the listing period.

- *Terms of Brokerage.* Is the brokerage exclusive, or will cobrokerage be acceptable? Will the property be listed on a multiple listing service (a very good idea)?

- *Broker's Priorities.* A clear statement as to who the broker will represent: the buyer, or the seller.

- *Miscellaneous Items.* Other areas covered are title insurance and escrow companies (which ones), arbitration (if you agree to it in a dispute), and who pays attorney fees if you go to court.

COMMISSION

Finally, there is that all important line in the listing agreement which specifies the commission, typically a percentage of the purchase price. Keep in mind that there is no "set" or "fixed" commission rate anywhere in the country. The commission is what you and your agent agree to. However, rates are usually 7 percent at the high end and 3 percent at the low end. A flat fee is sometimes also used.

 You can find agents who will work for low commissions, provided you do some of the work such as show the property and pay for advertising. In a strong market, this may be a good choice. In a weak market, it could lessen your chances for a quick sale. Some agents will refuse to take your listing unless you give them a "full" commission, typically 5 to 7 percent. It may be worth it to pay them what they want, if they are good and can produce a quick sale at a high price.

Beware of agents who want a high commission and a very long listing. They are telling you, in effect, that they don't anticipate finding a buyer any time soon, but they still want top dollar for their services.

In most areas, agents will list your property on a listing service regardless of the commission rate. However, it only stands to reason that agents might be more anxious to show properties with high commissions than with lower ones. (They are ethically required to show buyers the properties most suited to them, regardless of the commission rate.)

 Even though the listing agreement provides the brokerage commission, you can negotiate with the broker later on—especially if the broker is an independent and not part of a national organization. If, by reducing the commission a slight amount at your request, a sale takes place, the broker is ahead. Just don't be afraid to ask. The worst that will happen is that the broker will say no.

Chapter 8

How Do I Get Out of a Bad Listing Agreement?

There are a lot of reasons you might want to get out of a listing agreement. Some have to do with you, some with the broker's performance. Here are several:

- You put your house on the market, but your spouse does not approve. You now want to take it off the market.

- Two days after you listed your house at a price that the real estate broker thought was overly ambitious, you are swamped with offers. You now realize you're asking too little and you want to back out of the listing.

- After you list, you discover that even with $100,000 profit from a sale, you can't afford to live in the same neighborhood if you buy another house. Or, for that matter, any neighborhood near where you want to live, or have lived. Now you don't want to sell.

- The agent was very optimistic about getting a sale when you signed the listing agreement. But it's been two months and nobody's looked at the house. You think the agent isn't working hard for you and you want to get out of the listing agreement, so you can list with someone else.

- A week after you signed the listing, you had a fire in the attic and your home was seriously damaged. You don't want to sell until the insurance company pays off and everything is repaired.

These are all realistic nightmares that prospective sellers at one time or another have faced. You want to withdraw your listing. Yet, listings give the broker the right to find a buyer over a period of time and to collect a commission if successful. How do you get out of them without selling the house and paying that commission? Litigation is always a possibility. However, for reasons to be discussed, it should be considered the last choice in these situations. Negotiation with perhaps a bit of leverage is usually a far better solution.

THE COMMISSION

The only reason an agent takes a listing is to earn a commission. That commission is earned not when escrow actually closes, but when the agent delivers to you (based on a contractual agreement—a listing) a prospective buyer who is:

- Ready to purchase.
- Willing to purchase.
- Able to purchase.

Although the person may offer to buy the property, without introduction of any supplementary conditions, you don't actually have to sell. But, if the buyer is ready, willing, and able to purchase, you may owe a commission anyhow. The key here is the contractual arrangement you made with the broker by means of the listing. Without the listing (your agreement to pay a commission), you don't have to pay.

THE LISTING AGREEMENT

Thus, when you ask for the listing back, you are asking for the agent to give up on a potential future commission. If any time has passed since you signed the agreement, you're also asking the agent to overlook the efforts he or she has already made in finding a buyer. Needless to say, most agents do not look on this request with favor. However, you may get your listing back under a variety of technical circumstances:

- *Time.* Most agreements are for a specific period of time, for example, from April 1 through June 30. You can simply wait out the time period, then the listing expires and you're out of the obligation. (This is an excellent reason for giving a short-term listing, no more than 90 days.)
- *Special Circumstances.* Many listing provide that if something unusual happens, such as a fire at the premises or the death or serious illness of one the sellers, the listing is automatically terminated. If your listing has such a clause, you can refer to it. This is also something to ask for when you sign a listing agreement.

- *Lack of Performance.* Generally, listing agreements allow the agent to secure a buyer by whatever method he or she feels is reasonable. Some sellers, however, insist on a clause in the listing agreement that specifies the type of performance, for example, that the agent will advertise the property at least once a week in a specific newspaper with a specified minimum-size ad. The agent not advertising the property is cause for taking back the listing. (However, be sure the agent agrees with your decision, or you could end up in court.)

There is another way to get your listing back and that has to do with public relations. Most agents are very aware of their public image. The very last thing they want is any fuss with a seller that could result in bad publicity for them. This gives you some leverage (more or less depending on the agent).

Some of things you can do:

- Go to the local real estate board and file a complaint. If the agent truly has done something wrong, the board may apply pressure to have the listing returned. However, remember that it's up to the agent's discretion (in most cases) how to pursue finding a buyer and simply saying, "My broker hasn't worked hard enough!" isn't likely to get you much sympathy from other brokers.

- If the agent has done something that you think was unethical or even illegal, you can take the matter up with the state real estate board, which handles licensing. For example, one of your authors once knew an agent who, when soliciting business, would impress sellers by bringing potential buyers by to look at the property before and after signing the listing. It turned out, however, that the "prospective buyers" were actually members of the agent's family—aunts, uncles, and cousins—who did a pretend looking to help the agent get the listing and then keep it. One seller happened to know one of the people coming by and the scheme was unraveled. A letter to the state board pointing out this unethical conduct quickly got the listing back.

- Simply let the agent know how unhappy you are with the service and demand the listing back. Most agents don't want unhappy clients. Word gets out and soon it becomes difficult for the agent to get other listings. If you let the agent know how unhappy you are, he or she may simply realize it's not worth the hassle and return the listing to you. The exception here would be if you had the property listed very low, and the agent was convinced a sale could be quickly made. But, in that case, you might not want the listing back at all. Do not be tempted, in the waning days of a brokerage agreement's exclusivity, to suggest to a prospective buyer the possibility of coming back to you separately, after the exclusive period has expired. This almost always brings a lawsuit for a brokerage commission, and more often than not, the broker is highly successful. You can't use a broker to advertise property, and then attempt to cut the broker out of the commission.

WHAT IF THE HOUSE IS MISPRICED?

If it's too high, the broker will probably be happy to give you back the listing or negotiate for a lower price, since at the high price it's not going to sell anyway. If it's too low, the question becomes, how did it get priced that low? If the price is really out of line at the low end, the broker may readily agree with returning the listing, since in any lawsuit for a commission, the broker could be potentially liable for damages for a faulty appraisal. (You'd have to retain another broker or appraiser to be an expert, but that's another story.) If all else fails, a straightforward approach to the broker may be of some assistance. You may begin by telling the broker that the house is mispriced (and that you relied on them in setting it too low). You may then ask that they revise or return the listing agreement.

 If the price is out of line and, understandably, the broker easily finds a buyer, don't sign the sales agreement out of some misguided sense that you are obliged to do so. If you then fail to follow through on the sale, the buyer has a claim with specific performance, and damages; the broker, has a claim for commissions, and you will wind up defending two very expensive lawsuits (*Bregman v. Meehan,* 125 Misc. 2d 332, 479 N.Y.S.2d 422 (Sup. Nassau 1984)). What is clear is that if the matter isn't resolved quickly, you probably have need of professional counsel who can tell you the odds in a forthcoming law suit.

Chapter 9

Should I List or Sell My Home Myself?

Do I need a real estate broker to sell my home? No, you can sell it yourself. Do I need a real estate broker to find a buyer for my home? Probably. The statistics tell it all—upward of 90 percent of home sales are handled by agents. If it were so easy to do it yourself, chances are far more people would attempt it. That doesn't mean that you should simply forget about trying to sell your own home. Other than the decision to get married or divorced, the sale (or purchase) of a house is probably the biggest economic decision many of us make. In the course of the year, it is unlikely that most people write many checks above $10,000, yet the brokerage commission of a typical home selling for $200,000 will usually have a commission payable to the broker for more than that amount. If there were some way to save that money, wouldn't you be interested?

YOU DO THE WORK

It would be a mistake to think that there's no work involved in selling a home. Many people feel that the broker does little to earn a commission. He or she simply lists the house and then waits like a spider in a web for a prospective buyer to chance by. The broker brings you the buyer's offer, you sign, and then you owe this huge commission. That isn't the way it works. Brokers have huge expenses including advertising, automobile upkeep, office rent, legal fees, and insurance to name a few. They also have loads of experience. (Years ago, real estate brokers had the reputation of snake oil salesmen, but today, theirs is a highly professional operation—often computerized, and frequently involving great efforts to match prospective purchasers with property that is within their means, or perhaps just outside it.) You are paying for all this, even if you see little of it in operation.

WORK YOU'LL NEED TO DO

If you sell on your own, you must do the work that the broker does. Here's a list of things you'll need to do to save the commission:

- Procure and hang a sign in your front yard.
- Create a flyer to hang with the sign and to distribute at supermarket, drugstore, and similar outlet bulletin boards.
- Write an ad and pay for it to run every week in the local newspapers.
- Obtain a separate phone line or dedicate your current line to receiving messages from potential buyers. Get an answering machine so you won't miss any of them.
- Receive calls from buyers and "sell" them on seeing your home.
- Show potential buyers your house.
- Hold open houses.
- Receive offers, make counteroffers, and negotiate a deal.
- Handle all the paperwork including the sales agreement and escrow documents.
- Help the buyer secure financing.
- Clear title and have the deed prepared.
- Close escrow and sign all final escrow instructions.

Can you do it? Many people, particularly those who have been through real estate transactions in the past can. Once you've done it a couple of times, you'll see that it's really not that difficult.

GETTING HELP

If the task seems insurmountable to you, or if you put greater value on your own time, yet you still want to sell on your own, help is available. A number of real estate firms offer reduced rate commission in exchange for shared work. You pay for advertising and show the property and they will accept, for example, only a 3 percent commission. They'll handle all the paperwork and do some of the negotiating for you. Or, you can contact a real estate lawyer who for a very reasonable fee, usually under $1,000, will handle all the paperwork in the transaction. You just need to turn up a buyer who's ready, willing, and able to purchase.

 Time is money. The faster you can sell, the better it is for you, financially speaking. To speed up your sale, reduce your price by an amount almost equal to what you're saving by not paying a commission. The lower price will attract buyers and you'll get a quicker sale.

 If your house is being offered for $300,000, and it takes a year to sell, you may be better off putting it on the market for $275,000 and obtaining a buyer in six weeks.

The reason: You'll pay an $18,000 commission on average for the $300,000 residence, and you'll have to carry the place for a whole year (probable cost with a mortgage, property taxes, utilities, maintenance, insurance, and other items: another $25,000). On the $275,000 sale, your commission will average around $16,500 (a $1,500 savings) and assuming that you clear $200,000 after a mortgage is paid off, you can earn $16,000 or more in interest—and not have to pay $25,000 in carrying costs.

PROBLEMS AREAS TO WATCH OUT FOR

If you sell by owner, there are going to be some difficult paths you'll have to tread. You'll want to be on the alert to be sure that you don't stumble and fall:

- *Sales Agreement.* It needs to be drawn correctly to protect you and to be a legally binding document. Once you have the buyer in hand, have your attorney draw it up.
- *Disclosure Forms.* Your state may have a prescribed form that you must give to the buyers. Check with a local real estate broker.
- *Negotiating.* It's a lot easier to negotiate through a third party, the broker, than to do it yourself face-to-face with the buyers. Be prepared to compromise, sometimes more than you'd like, to keep the buyers happy and moving forward with the sale.
- *Clearing Title.* You'll have to be sure that all documents are obtained in order for you to give clear title. This may mean getting signed "satisfaction of payment" forms from lien holders or other

documents. Be sure you check with the escrow officer to see exactly what's needed.

- *Closing Documents.* Unless you're very familiar with real estate deals, have an attorney check these over for you. There is nothing to legally prevent you from selling your own house. Many people do it. However, it is trickier than just going to the store and buying a can of soda. Our best advice is that if you've been through real estate transactions before, you might want to give it a try. If this is your first sale, definitely let a broker and attorney handle it.

Chapter 10

Should I "Counteroffer"?

Law students typically spend more than six months in their law school contracts course studying the concepts of "offer," "acceptance," and "counteroffer," and mastering the procedure for creating a binding agreement between the parties. It is an apocryphal story that those who study it hardest and longest become the law school professors who teach it to the next generation. Those who study it a bit less, and understand it not quite as well, become the judges who interpret the offers written by the successful lawyers who don't understand it at all, but have the ability to find clients with whom to practice law.

Nowhere is a counteroffer more prevalent than in real estate transactions where the seller offers the premises at a fixed price and the buyer wants a different price and set of conditions.

COUNTERING

Prospective buyers who would like to become owners have a choice. They can accept the offer to sell by the purchaser, without change, go to contract and make a purchase, or they can propose minor (or major) changes in the hope that a seller will agree.

When as a buyer you offer anything other than exactly what the seller is asking in terms of price and conditions, you are in effect, counteroffering. This is done on a form which goes by several names including "Sales Agreement," "Purchase Offer," and "Deposit Receipt." Typically, it includes all of the terms the buyers want as well as the price. If the sellers are agreeable to all of the conditions proposed by the buyers including price, they can accept and it's a done deal. That rarely happens. Typically, the sellers want a higher price and different terms. Therefore, they now counter the buyer's offer.

This can go back and forth with buyers and sellers countering as many times as both parties are willing to keep the negotiations alive. One of your authors has seen as many as a dozen counteroffers in a single deal that was finally signed by all.

Eventually, when both parties are finally in complete agreement, a contract is formed.

Note that the process involves negotiations going along with documentation. Rarely do real estate transactions occur with a handshake followed by the paperwork. Most often the paperwork forms the offer and signing concludes the contract.

PRICE AND TERMS

What is most common in counteroffers is a change in price. For example, the seller wants $199,000 for a home, the buyer wants to pay $160,000. Even if the parties agree on every other issue and term, no contract can be formed because of this fundamental disagreement.

Terms are also important. These can range from having the seller carry-back some financing to an engineering report to a series of representations by the seller, such as "The roof shall be free of leaks at the time of the closing." It can also contain mortgage contingency clauses and other modifications that are routinely agreed to in an otherwise handshake deal.

Often there is a trade-off between terms and price. One party gets their price while the other gets more favorable terms.

PREPARING THE COUNTEROFFER

In most parts of the country, real estate agents will prepare offers and counteroffers. In the past they would actually write out much of the text of the offer in longhand and then have everyone sign. However, since these agents were not attorneys, often the language was not sufficiently accurate to allow the contract to be upheld in court. A series of cases across the country where agent-drawn contracts were not upheld led to the current version of the "sales agreement" that most agents use.

While it will differ from office to office, typically it's as much as a dozen pages long and everything in it has been prepared in advance by lawyers. All that need be added is the names of the parties, the address of the property and the price. Even contingency clauses and provisions for financing have their own paragraph. If they apply, they are simply checked and initialed by all parties.

The advantage of the almost totally boilerplate contract is that there is far less chance of it being drawn incorrectly. On the other hand, there's also far less flexibility if something should arise that the creators of the contract did not foresee. In these circumstances, the agent may scribble in the unexpected terms or conditions . . . and in so doing may inadvertently weaken the contract.

Ideally, an attorney would prepare the sales agreement/offer/counteroffer specifically for the transaction involved. In real life, however, attorneys often do exactly what the agents do. The attorney gets a standard form (often created in computers) and prints out the sales agreement/offer/counteroffer. Only if necessary do they then add a paragraph or two that might be specific to the particular transaction.

CAN YOU DO IT YOURSELF?

Certainly, if you're aware of the risks. Boilerplate sales agreements/offers/counteroffers are readily available. We've even included one in this book (see Appendix). You can take it to your attorney to have him or her make it specific to your transaction (and the laws of your state). Or, if you're sufficiently knowledgeable, you can do it yourself.

One alternative is an informal (non-binding) agreement between buyer and sellers that uses the following form letter:

Dear Seller:

I have viewed your house at (street location) and wish to make a formal bid for the same. I offer to purchase this, subject to the usual terms and conditions of a contract, with mortgage and _____ contingencies, for $_____.

Please let me hear from you concerning this in the next two days.

Cordially,

If differences in terms and price can be ironed out and the seller accepts with a handshake, both buyer and seller can then go to a real estate attorney who can prepare the paperwork. (Remember, the attorney's fee in these cases is often under $1,000 and that's for handling the entire transaction.)

BINDING AGREEMENT

It's important to understand that while all of the negotiating goes on—the series of counteroffers, counterproposals, and discussions—

neither party is bound to the deal nor is there an agreement. The heart of the contract is the purchase price. The negotiations—sometimes between lawyers, other times involving the real estate broker and one or more of the parties—to refine the purchase price through counteroffers do not bind the parties. In fact, until both buyers and sellers are in uniform agreement (a meeting of the minds), which is then reduced to a written *and signed* contract, either party can simply walk away. You are not bound by a proposal . . . until the other side accepts it, exactly as offered.

TYPICAL CONTENTS OF COUNTEROFFERS

Counteroffers can contain almost anything. Here are a few of the terms, in addition to price, most frequently found:

- Change in price.
- Mortgage contingency, both as to the amount of the mortgage, length (duration in years, typically 15 or 30 years) of the mortgage, the rate and time under which to obtain a mortgage a mortgage commitment (anywhere from 30 to 90 days).
- The date of the closing. Usually the stipulation is that if the buyer can't procure the mortgage, the deal is canceled and buyer gets back the deposit.
- The amount of time prior to, or subsequent to the closing that the seller will vacate the premises.
- Whether the buyer will be permitted to store items at the premises prior to the closing (most lawyers recommend against it) or have access to the premises (most lawyers will permit it if the seller is indemnified).
- What light fixtures will remain at the premises? Typical fixtures that are removed are dining room fixtures or crystal chandeliers, but there is no set rule.
- What pending tax assessments (if any) are to be apportioned?
- Whether the contract of sale may be assigned to someone else.
- Whether the mortgage on the parcel is assignable or assumable.
- What repairs or replacements seller is willing to effect in the event a building inspector or engineer finds defect.

It's important to consider what you are willing to bind yourself to do in the contract. The reason is that once it is signed, and if it is properly drawn, it is virtually cast in stone and not changeable.

 If you make your house sale subject to an engineering report, or a building inspection, and agree to cure defects that are found, limit yourself to a dollar amount.

It's not unreasonable for a buyer of a $200,000 home to demand that you spend up to $500 to fix broken windows, an attic fan, or a hot water heater. It is less than reasonable to demand that you replace the old central air conditioning system that died after the contract was signed, but before the building inspection was completed. You can do this with the following clause added to the contract:

> Subject to an engineering report and the repairs that the same calls for, provided such repairs do not exceed $500 in the aggregate. If such repairs cost more, seller may do so at his or her own expense, or if unwilling to do so, and if buyer will not assume cost of same or waive such repair, seller may cancel the contract without further liability to the buyer.

In the final analysis, virtually everything is negotiable in a realty contract—and a solution can be had at a certain price. The question is whether buyer, or seller, is willing to pay it.

Chapter 11

Should I Consider a Lease-Option to Help Sell My Home?

"When times are tough, the tough get going!" Or at least, so goes the old maxim. When times get tough in real estate, however, sellers begin thinking about the lease-option. Its most common use is as an alternative to selling a home in a weak market.

As its name implies, this is a hybrid contract. Part of it is a standard lease—tenants agree to rent the premises for a specified period for a certain sum of money (and all the clauses that go with the lease). Another part, however, is an "option to purchase." Here the sellers agree to sell the property to prospective buyers at a future date, *at the option of the buyers*. At the future date, the would-be buyers can choose to purchase, or not by exercising the option to purchase.

HOW IT WORKS

Originally a lease-option was designed to provide a means for a buyer without a down payment to purchase a home. The buyer would lease the property and during the time of the lease, a portion of the money paid as rent would be informally set aside each month toward the down payment. (Usually the rent is set higher than the going rate for such property.) When the prospective buyers had accumulated sufficient funds for the down payment, they could exercise their option and complete the purchase. When the real estate market is weak, sellers offer this same enticement to try to convert tenants to buyers.

PROS AND CONS FOR THE BUYER/LESSEE/OPTIONEE

- *Pro.* Get a long-term lease, typically from two to five years.
- *Pro.* Tie up a piece of property at a set price (usually).

- *Pro.* Set in place a mechanism of forced savings to help accumulate the down payment.
- *Con.* May lose the property (or wind up in litigation) if the seller renegs on the option.
- *Con.* Paying higher than market rent.
- *Con.* Property may not maintain value in a falling market, meaning that when it's time to exercise the option and buy, the property could be worth far less than the option price.

PROS AND CONS FOR SELLER/LESSOR/OPTIONOR

- *Pro.* Get immediate income from the property.
- *Pro.* Get higher rent than the market would otherwise bear.
- *Pro.* Get a sale, albeit years in the future.
- *Con.* Buyer/tenant may not be able to make payments and may leave.
- *Con.* Disgruntled buyer/tenant may vandalize property before leaving.
- *Con.* Property is tied up so that in event prices go higher, you're committed to a lower price by the option.

For the protection of the buyer/tenant, the lease-option should be recorded, thus giving constructive notice of the buyer/tenant's position in the property and preventing the seller/landlord from otherwise disposing of it.

WHAT USUALLY HAPPENS

Lease-options either work very well or very badly with very little middle ground. In a good lease option, the buyer/tenant will pay the rent, the seller/landlord will credit a large portion of that rent toward a down payment and, eventually, the buyer/tenant will use that credit to help make the purchase.

In a bad lease/option, usually not enough of the rent is credited toward the down payment and eventually the buyer/tenant realizes that the hope of purchasing the property is in reality nothing more than wishful thinking. Or, the buyers/tenants get ready to buy and discover that they can't qualify for a sufficient mortgage to complete the purchase, and thus lose their accumulated down payment. Or the buyers/tenants over the course of the lease/option period become ill, lose jobs, or otherwise find they can no longer make the payments and quit.

WHAT TO LOOK FOR IN A LEASE-OPTION

Generally speaking a lease-option should include the following:

- The full term of the lease (from date to date).
- The full amount of the money to be paid under the lease.
- The monthly amount and the place to be paid.
- The amount of the monthly payment that is to go toward the down payment.
- The full purchase price and terms of purchase.
- The option statement (buyers have the option of purchasing said property at said price on said terms at said date provided monthly payments have been made according to terms and so on). In order for it to be an enforceable contract, there must be some form of consideration paid by the buyer/tenant/optionee to the seller/landlord/optionor for the option. This can be in the form of either a lump sum paid at the beginning, or it can be the monthly amount credited toward the down payment. Either way, it should be stipulated in the lease option agreement.

 If you want to buy the property, get qualified for a mortgage of the amount you'll need at the time you sign the lease/option. True, by the time you exercise the option, interest rates will have changed and your income could have gone up or down as well. But at least you'll know that you potentially can qualify for the necessary mortgage.

 If you're the landlord/seller, qualify the buyer/tenant as you would any other renter. Check a credit report, bank statement and with previous landlords. Get a hefty security deposit. Don't be so blinded by the thought of the sale, that you let a bad tenant into your property.

CAN A SELLER/LESSOR/OPTIONOR
FORCE THE OTHER PARTY TO BUY?

No. The buyer/lessee/optionee has the option to buy or not. But you can enforce the terms of the lease as with any other tenant.

CAN A BUYER/LESSEE/OPTIONEE
GET OUT OF THE AGREEMENT?

Yes and no. Yes, you can get out of the option easily enough by just not exercising it. The lease is another matter. If you truly didn't understand what was involved when you signed, can't make the higher-than-market payments or realize that you'll never accumulate the needed down payment in time under the terms, you can go to small claims court for relief. For the most part, tenants who have the financial need to break a lease are going to find that the landlord wants them gone. Landlords really only want the rent, not the headache associated with collecting it.

 It may cost you a month's security, but you can try asking your landlord to let you out of the lease, and to rerent the property. Or, you can undertake renting it yourself and present the landlord with a new, ideal tenant. If the landlord doesn't agree to the change, it will be hard to argue that he has been damaged—all he has done is fail to mitigate potential damage. Again, to avoid litigation, a small payment may buy you your peace.

Getting a New Mortgage

Chapter 12

What Is a Mortgage?

Every mortgage is a contract, and a security agreement, designed to assure a lender in a secured transaction that the borrower will repay the debt on penalty of losing the property pledged to ensure the integrity of the obligor. In short, you put up the property, the lender puts up the money. Technically, it's called a pledge or "hypothecation." You give up the property, yet you don't give up the right to use it . . . unless you fail to make the payments. Then the lender can take the property from you. A good way to start is with the premise that a mortgage is a one-sided instrument, primarily intended to benefit, and give rights to the mortgagee (the lender).

In a different sense, you and the bank are partners in a real estate venture, only it is a very senior-junior partnership. The bank has the rights, and you have the liability (namely, the debts and a series of covenants that you must comply with). Typical covenants or clauses that warrant you will do something are found in a mortgage under which the borrower promises to make payments promptly to the mortgagee (the lender).

Nearly all mortgages have a "grace period," which calls for payments to be made by a certain date each month, but allow you some short period of time thereafter to make payments. Sometimes the period is as short as 5 days, sometimes as long as 15 days, but a failure to make payment by the conclusion of the grace period is an act of default. That can bring about dire consequences under the mortgage.

It is always important to read the terms and conditions of the mortgage properly and ascertain just how the bank calculates your balance. On second mortgages, the bank may not have a grace period at all. However, they may not apply a penalty to the account unless more than 5 or 15 days or some other limit in days have passed. The reason for this is that on many mortgages, interest continues to accrue on the unpaid principal balance until it is actually paid. That applies to when the check is paid by your bank—not necessarily when it is deposited.

The value of your money counts. If you keep your funds in a day of deposit–day of withdrawal money market account earning just 3 percent, the amount of interest earned on a daily basis is about eight cents per day per thousand dollars of mortgage payment. On a $7,500 payment, that amounts to $18.49 a month.

 If your bank does measure interest based on when it is paid, regardless of the grace period, then you really need to measure the value of your money. Suppose you are paying off your mortgage with a 15-day grace period before a late fee is imposed. A provision states that interest is calculated on the unpaid balance, and on a mortgage of $150,000 at 9 percent interest; therefore each day that the mortgage remains unpaid adds about $37 in interest to the overall cost of the loan (the balance of the monthly payments is principal reduction). Thus, instead of mailing your check by ordinary mail to the bank, which might take 3 or 4 days to arrive—at a cost of about $100 to you—it actually pays to spend $11 for Express Mail. The reason: when it arrives fully, you save 3 days worth of interest, in this case about $100, which goes straight to your bottom line. Other typical clauses found in a mortgage include:

- A covenant to pay your taxes on time (some banks collect $1/12$ per month of your taxes in advance, and make the payments for you).
- A covenant to maintain the premises in good repair.
- A covenant to keep the premises insured (the mortgagee is almost always named as a loss payee in the event of a loss by fire, flood, or other damage).
- The entire amount of the then-remaining indebtedness becomes due on the sale of the premises.

Whether the security instrument is a mortgage, or a deed of trust, the concept is the same: The bank has to be secured, and it takes a belt-and-suspenders approach; the more security it has, the more comforting it feels, and usually the more it is willing to lend. When a bank makes a loan that it intends to resell into the secondary mortgage market, it almost always will utilize a loan drawn in accordance with the guidelines of the Federal National Mortgage Association (FNMA, or Fannie Mae) the terms of which are not negotiable, or variable.

If you spot a comma that is out of place, you will be commended for your proofreading ability, but the instrument will not be changed. This is because a legion of investors knows precisely what the Fannie Mae mortgages look like, and exactly how it will be interpreted by the course of law.

Mortgages that do not conform to the Fannie Mae guidelines may be issued by the bank; however, this forms a "portfolio" loan of the bank that cannot be privatized into a security without a significant amount of work by the bank (generally speaking, not worth it). In essence, the mortgage becomes a commercial loan—all the terms of which are generally speaking highly negotiable.

Even though the mortgage is secured by land and improvements on that land, it is also enforceable by your personal promise to pay. If you default, the mortgagee has the right to elect to bring a judicial claim against you based on the mortgage, which is foreclosed on, or the bond or note which may be sued on. If the premises are foreclosed on and sold, and the mortgagee does not receive the full amount of the mortgage, plus all interest and penalties accrued, then there is a right to undertake deficiency proceedings. Once the foreclosure is completed, the note or bond which also collateralizes the loan is extinguished.

An exception here is that many states offer protection if the loan is a "purchase money mortgage." That means that the loan was part of the purchase price whether the lender was the seller or a bank. In states with such laws, no deficiency judgment may be rendered on a purchase money mortgage. There are many other clauses in mortgages; all of them have some importance. When you look at a mortgage before signing, be sure that the following are in order:

- Amount of the loan.
- Duration of payment (15 years, 30 years, or some other time frame).
- Monthly payment that you'll be making.
- Whether there's a pickup for taxes and other expenses.
- Rate of interest being charged.
- If you have a right to assign the mortgage, that this appears in the document.
- If you have an adjustable rate mortgage, how the rate adjusts; if not, that the loan is in fact fixed. If you read only that, although there are other clauses and requirements, you've found the essence of the transaction, which covers these major points.

Chapter 13

How Can I Save Money
on My Mortgage?

"Neither a borrower, nor a lender be." William Shakespeare put it best four centuries ago in defining what would become an American virtue. And although Americans do not have one of the world's highest rates of private saving, they do have the highest incidence of private residence ownership. One of the key reasons is the availability of capital for mortgages, and a tax structure that encourages private home ownership. Thus, most Americans, with deference to Shakespeare, have become borrowers of enormous sums of mortgage money.

Buying a home is typically the largest single investment that most people make, and the largest type of financial transaction in a lifetime. As part of it, the mortgage is inevitably the largest financial obligation that an individual undertakes.

GETTING A MORTGAGE

Applying for a mortgage is pretty much like inviting someone into your bedroom to look at your underwear drawer. For a man, it's not a pretty sight. For a woman, it's akin to allowing a stranger to rummage through that drawer. Still, with some careful advance planning, you can make the experience, relatively speaking, pleasurable, short, and one that saves you a substantial amount of money over the long run. Here are some money-saving ideas that you may want to consider when you apply for a mortgage, or for refinancing your existing mortgage loan:

- First, decide what type of loan suits you best. A fixed rate mortgage? An adjustable rate mortgage (called an ARM)? A blended mortgage that is fixed for a period of years and then switches to an adjustable rate? Or even a boutique loan that is especially tailored to your economic situation and overall goals?

Some simple clues to saving money are, when interest rates are low, go for a fixed rate mortgage and lock in those low rates. When interest rates are high, consider an ARM that starts with a low rate and hope to refinance a few years down the road when interest rates (hopefully) drop.

- Second, look at the loan term. The longest term usually offers the highest rates. If you can pay off your loan in 15 years instead of 30, generally speaking, you can save ½ to 1 percent in the interest rate. Sometimes you can have the best of both worlds. You can get a mortgage whose monthly payment is substantially lowered because it is calculated as if you would pay it off in 30 years, even though it has a "balloon payment" that is due in full in 3, 5, 7, or 10 years. This may also save upward of a percentage point in interest—but be prepared to refinance or sell the property before that balloon payment is due. Simply by way of example, a 15-year loan of $100,000 at 10 percent is amortized on a self-liquidating mortgage at the rate of $1,074.61 per month. At the end of five years, there is a balance of $81,316 due on the loan. By going to a 30-year payment plan with a five-year balloon, the monthly carrying cost drops to $877.57, but at the end of 60 months, there's still a balance of $96,574 owed on the loan.

- Consider a "convertible" mortgage. This loan starts as an ARM, then after a specified period of time, usually, 3 to 5 years, it converts to a fixed rate—at your option. If interest rates are high, you can start as an ARM and then when (and if) they drop, convert to a fixed rate to lock them in without the additional costs of refinancing.

- Talk to a mortgage broker about the different types of mortgages available at the time you need one. There are literally hundreds of different types from which to choose. Some come into existence, last a few months, and disappear. Maybe one of these will be just right for you. Mortgage brokers are listed as such in the Yellow Pages.

EXTRA MONEY-SAVING IDEAS

Here are some unusual ways to save money when making mortgage payments:

When applying for a loan, ask whether the lender will allow you to make payments biweekly, rather than monthly. Over the lifetime of the mortgage, this can save you a substantial amount. On a $100,000 mortgage, payable over 30 years, the monthly payment would be $877.50. If you make biweekly payments of $438.75 and each payment is applied directly to your mortgage, instead of 720 payments (360 × 2) you will only have to make 566 payments. The difference: 134 payments ($58,792) stays in your pocket. And, your mortgage is paid off in about 22 years instead of 30 years.

Make certain that you have the right to prepay the mortgage in whole or in part at any time. This will allow you to make an additional payment each month, perhaps as little as $50. It may not sound like much, but over the lifetime of the mortgage, the savings are substantial. By simply adding $50 monthly (not biweekly) on a $100,000 loan at 10 percent, you can have the mortgage paid in 275 months, rather than 360.

Even if you just add $20 a month to your 30-year mortgage (of $100,000 at 10 percent interest), instead of 360 payments, you can reduce them to 318 payments. The savings from 42 payments: almost $37,000.

If you are self-employed, or have significant undocumented income, applying for a mortgage is almost always a problem. However, you can save time, money, and effort if you ask whether or not the lending institution has a no-income verification policy. This is usually available for people who have the best credit, and can substantially eliminate many of the problems.

If you have a low income, but a high property valuation, "No-income mortgages," with asset verification, are sometimes available. These can substantially eliminate many of the problems associated with trying to show that you meet the underwriting guidelines for income in conforming loans.

If you do not qualify for a no-income check, but have substantial assets, say, an IRA or retirement account, ask the lender if they have an "asset verification mortgage." This allows them to verify that you have sums on deposit, even though you may not presently be able to draw on them without substantial tax penalty. It cuts down on your paperwork, and even though there may be a small interest premium over a fully documented mortgage, the time that you save may be substantial—and if you value your time, that may be worthwhile.

WHAT TO DO TO GET STARTED

If you want (or need) a mortgage, start a file as quickly as possible and keep a chronological record of correspondence, and of all documents that you send to the lender, or to the mortgage broker. Contact a variety of lender's agents including banks and mortgage brokers. But avoid committing to any of them. You commit when you sign papers and give them money. Until then, you can simply walk away and try somewhere else. Prepare an application.

It's best if you ask a lender's agent for an application that is used for "conforming loans," those that meet the underwriting guidelines of Fannie Mae or Freddie Mac, the semiofficial organizations that finance the loan you get to the lender. This is a standard form and if you fill it out once and make copies, you can submit it many times without having to go through the trouble to fill another form out again from scratch.

- Beware of agreeing to pay points up front. (A "point" is 1 percent of the mortgage amount. On a $100,000 mortgage three points equal $3,000.) Shop around. You may find a lender who charges fewer points or no points. (Generally, the lower the points, however, the higher the interest rate and vice versa.)

- Don't be trapped by thinking that you'll live in your home forever and, hence, you must get the most expensive loan because it has the most long-term benefits. Remember, most people move on the average once every seven to nine years, and that probably includes you. You may not intend moving today, but by tomorrow your circumstances and inclinations may change.

- Beware of "garbage fees," the extra costs (such as document recording fees, and undetermined "lender's fees") that lenders tack on, often to make up for lower points or interest rate. These fees can easily amount to 1 percent or more of the mortgage amount. Check around with different lenders to see who will give you the best deal.

Chapter 14

Should I Use a Mortgage Broker?

A mortgage broker can be very much like a best friend: always there for you. Mortgage brokers come in all shapes and sizes. From individuals to corporations, they perform their functions securing both financing and refinancing for residential and commercial property purchases. Their activities are regulated, they are compensated for their service, and if you use a good one, they can save you a lot of money in the long run.

WHERE TO FIND A MORTGAGE BROKER

Mortgage brokers function best where there is a large concentration of capital available for lending on real estate transactions. Typically, this surrounds large standard metropolitan statistical areas (SMSA) and most probably could be found in or around any city with a population of 500,000 people or more. (One or two are always available in small communities, even in rural areas.) If you are not acquainted with one, here are some good sources that you might wish to consider:

- Yellow Pages (under Mortgage Brokers).
- Sunday newspaper—Finance and Real Estate Sections.
- Recommendation from your local real estate agent.
- Recommendation or word of mouth from your friends.
- National Mortgage Brokers Association Referral Service.
- Local Better Business Bureau.

PREQUALIFYING

Perhaps the single most important function that a mortgage broker can accomplish is to prequalify you for a loan. What this means is that the broker will examine your income stream (gross income, your debts, and assets) and your credit history, and attempt to ascertain the best type of loan for you. The mortgage broker is able to do this because most mortgages offered by banks and savings and loans today (as well as much privately funded money from sources such as insurance companies) must meet underwriting guidelines established by the Federal National Mortgage Association (FNMA or "Fannie Mae").

If the borrower does not meet the underwriting guidelines, then the lender cannot resell the loan on the secondary market and must "eat" it itself. It becomes what is known in the trade as a "portfolio loan." The mortgage broker usually starts by ascertaining the amount that you can comfortably pay, each month, as part of your monthly payment, and then works backward, by extrapolation, to determine what the loan principal will be, and what its repayment term can manage.

Mortgage brokers are generally skilled at ascertaining whether a fixed or variable-rate loan is wise, whether a 15-, 20-, or 30-year loan is appropriate, and whether your mortgage loan needs to be large enough to cover closing costs, or if these costs can be minimized. Mortgage brokers can specialize in primary (first mortgage) or secondary financing, or even finding some unusual type of coverage such as a "wraparound" mortgage over existing financing. More imaginative financing is undertaken in states like New York, which place a tax on each mortgage recorded, but not on consideration already paid.

 If there's an existing mortgage of $100,000 and you need $110,000 in loans to buy the house, if you can assume the existing mortgage you need only add $10,000 in consideration. If you can assume the mortgage in New York, you save $2,000 in mortgage recording fees (you only pay on the new consideration of $10,000—not the $100,000 that remains in place by assumption, modification, consolidation, or extension). Significant in terms of how a mortgage can be placed is the creditworthiness of the applicant. Most mortgage brokers will ask you for permission to run a credit check, and then suggest, if the credit is less than stellar, that there may be alternative means by which you can still get a loan.

 If you are low on cash, but have a significant amount of money in an individual retirement account or Keogh plan, an asset verification loan might be worth considering. Even though the IRA or Keogh may not be utilized by the lender in the event of default, you could use it subject to paying the various penalties. Most lenders charge a little more for this, but would give someone otherwise without credit the opportunity to own their own home, or even to lower their interest rate.

 "No-income" loans (meaning loans on which your income is not verified) are frequently available to individuals purchasing property who pay more than 25 percent of the purchase price as a down payment, after closing costs. The bank's theory is that with that much equity involved, you won't jeopardize your home. Again, the rate of interest is usually a little bit higher for this than for a conventional loan, but it can be viable.

 A "no-income check, asset verification loan" is a hybrid of these two, often with a different rate of interest. Most mortgage brokers, if you ask them, will shop for the lowest rates available for you. Sometimes, however, their commission depends on their volume so it is always important to compare rates with the rates of others that are lending in the marketplace.

 Ask your mortgage broker about no-point options. The interest rate will be slightly higher—sometimes considerably—but if you're strapped for cash, the small increase in the monthly payments that you pay could be a better deal than two or three points charged up front. On a $100,000 loan, three points is equal to $3,000. By contrast, the difference between 8 percent and 8½ percent on a self-liquidated, self-amortized loan of $100,000, repayable on a monthly basis, is $35 each month. It would take 85 months (or just a bit more than seven years) to make back the $3,000 (longer if you count the interest). So, if you think you'll trade houses within seven years or so, or are cash short, and you can avoid points by going just a half point or so higher, why not go for it?

WHAT TO WATCH OUT FOR

Beware of heavy fees from the mortgage broker. Usually they are "retailers" who secure mortgages wholesale from lenders. In other words, the lenders pay their fees. If you go to a bank, the loan may be

8 percent at two points. A mortgage broker should charge no more. Instead, he or she is being compensated by the bank for finding a suitable borrower. Some mortgage brokers, however, add on extra fees. Comparison shop between mortgage brokers and retail lenders. Remember, money is money. If you can get the same amount from a bank or savings and loan at a lower interest rate with fewer points, there's no advantage in paying more.

Chapter 15

Do I Need a Lawyer When Getting a Second Mortgage (or Home Equity Loan)?

Probably not. Look at your house like a bank account. If you've owned it for a while, you've built up some equity that you can tap for a variety of purposes. Perhaps for your child's tuition, or for a wedding or even for an addition to the premises. The way you get it out, without selling, is to give someone a second (or higher) mortgage. You get the cash and the obligation to pay back. Unless the second mortgage transaction is particularly unusual—suppose that your house has an unusual covenant and restriction that runs with the land, or there's a proposed street widening that will go right through your dining room—or the laws in your state so provide, the odds are strong that you can handle a second mortgage transaction yourself, if you are willing to do some legwork.

It reminds one of the authors of the time that an inspiration struck to install a storm door at the rear of his residence. He purchased the door, and a full day's work later, had installed it almost perfectly. Sears advertised the door, *completely installed,* in the following week's newspaper for just $10 more than its original cost. As a carpenter, the $10-a-day wages might not have been worth it, but the sense of self-satisfaction was. And this may also prove true for a refinance or second mortgage on your residence.

WHAT IS A SECOND MORTGAGE?

A second mortgage is a "subordinated obligation," meaning that the first mortgage (the original loan on the premises) comes first in time. That's really fairly simple to understand. If you default on the first mortgage, and the lender forecloses, it can wipe out the second mortgage in its entirety. Therefore, there is more risk involved to a lender of a second mortgage and rates are usually somewhat higher than a first mortgage. Second mortgages also are usually for a shorter duration—15 years, 10 years, 5 years, or less—rather than the 30-year loans that many homeowners utilize when they are first buying a home to live in.

Also second mortgages can go by the term "home equity" loans. These are usually nothing more than straight second mortgages. However, they may have some additional protection for you. Second mortgages can be for either a fixed rate or an adjustable rate, as in the case of many home equity loans. With adjustable rate second mortgages, the interest rate and the payments may fluctuate greatly over the term of the loan. Finally, some home equity loans are actually "revolving" loans. For a period of time, typically 10 years or so, after they are obtained, you can withdraw funds up to a maximum amount. You can then pay back any amount you've withdrawn without penalty, and later withdraw the funds again. You only pay interest on the money you've actually withdrawn.

APPLYING FOR A SECOND MORTGAGE

Unlike applying for the original mortgage, a second lien or mortgage on your residence won't usually have all the underwriting guidelines and income verification requirements. The lender's biggest concern will be on the worth of your residence. The reason is that the lender will want to be assured that you have sufficient equity to justify making a loan. Most bank home equity (second mortgage) loans require that you have more than 20 percent equity, although some will accept less. They will lend the difference between the minimum required equity and what you actually have. For example, if you have 35 percent equity and they require a minimum of 20 percent, they will lend you 15 percent of your home's value.

REQUIREMENTS

Here are some of the likely requirements that you'll have to meet before you can successfully apply for a second mortgage:

- You'll have to make sure that there are no judgments outstanding against you; if you have any judgments against you, they have to be cleaned up—paid before closing. (The proceeds can typically be utilized to pay off the judgment.)

- Any back taxes against the property have to be paid and brought current.
- Your insurance policies (homeowners, fire) will have to be amended to name the second lender as an additional loss payee, as their interest may appear.
- If you've added on to your home, you'll probably need a certificate of occupancy to reflect the addition.
- Most likely, you'll need a survey to show the bank or finance company the legal description of the parcel.
- You'll probably need your income tax returns for the past two or three years, to show the bank your income.
- You'll have to sign a promissory note and a mortgage or deed of trust to secure the bank or finance company. Many banks prepare second mortgage documents on their own, using forms approved by their counsel. These so-called boilerplate forms can be prepared by a paralegal, or even a nonlawyer, and are relatively safe to sign as long as you read the material terms and are satisfied with them.

Helpful Hint   Banks can and do make mistakes when they prepare their own documents. In one case, a leading commercial bank in New York City made a loan to a customer in Connecticut that was intended to be a first mortgage on his residence. The employee preparing the loan document picked up the wrong forms, using those for a second mortgage. A court (where the borrower was sued by the lender of a multimillion dollar loan) ultimately decided that the second mortgage form was in fact a first mortgage, but it proved to be a very expensive lesson for all concerned. So be certain what it is that you sign (*In re Rundlett,* 136 B.R. 376 (S.D.N.Y. 1992); related proceedings 142 B.R. 649 and 142 B.R. 655 (S.D.N.Y. 1992)).

WHAT TO LOOK FOR

Here are some handy hints about your mortgage loan:

Helpful Hint   Make sure you read and understand the entire agreement. If you don't, you could sign up for a loan that could jeopardize the ownership of your home. If you're uncertain, worried, or just don't know, seek professional assistance.

Helpful Hint Material items that you should consider—and be certain you are happy with—include the amount of the mortgage or lien; the amount of the monthly payment; any additional requirements such as penalties for late payment, "due on sale" clauses for the balance of the mortgage, or other prohibitions.

Helpful Hint The title report which will point out defects that may exist. The bank can also prepare affidavits for you to sign if the title company comes up with possible judgments against someone with a name similar to yours. (You probably signed something similar at the time that you first bought the property.)

Helpful Hint If you're getting an adjustable rate mortgage, be sure you understand what affects the interest rate and payments. Often ARMs are tied to the cost of funds for the lender, which then adds a margin to them to come up with your monthly interest charge. There may also be a minimum payment.

Don't be surprised if the bank wants proof of your identity at the time of the closing of the second mortgage. A driver's license or passport is typically okay for this. The reason: Sometimes there have been fraudulent "owners" who have signed mortgages and other agreements, and then left the bank in the lurch. If you don't have proof and have to leave to get it and you have a lawyer (who is being paid by the hour), he or she cleans up at your expense. Avoid it!

OPPORTUNITIES

Here are some opportunities that you shouldn't pass up in considering a mortgage:

Helpful Hint Don't overlook the possibility of using a second mortgage to replace a small first mortgage, particularly if the rate is right. Generally speaking, second mortgages are much easier to qualify for.

Helpful Hint So long as the second mortgage received by you, together with the existing lien, doesn't exceed the original purchase price, with a very few exceptions, this will entitle you to take the full mortgage deduction on your income tax, provided the amount of the second mortgage does not exceed $100,000. There are some complicated rules involving this, but your accountant can do it properly (or, you can look at the instructions on the standard IRS Form 1040 next April 15).

 You may be able to refinance an existing loan for less than the cost of a second mortgage. Consider this as an alternative. If you refinance in a jurisdiction that taxes mortgages that are recorded, think about having your first mortgage assigned, consolidated, and extended to form a first lien. You can save thousands of dollars in mortgage recording taxes this way.

Foreclosure

Chapter 16

What Is Foreclosure? Should I Use It if a Borrower Doesn't Pay Up on a Mortgage I Hold?

Foreclosure is a remedy that is typically undertaken by a lender against a borrower who is the owner of one or more parcels of real property that are used as security for the loan. The lender hasn't been paid, and wants to be. So the lender wants to have the collateral for the loan sold off to satisfy the debt.

No national statute governs the foreclosure of real property, per se, though several national statutes do have applicability. Instead, each of the 50 states, and the District of Columbia, have local statutes governing foreclosure and sale; these typically are found in local codes that regulate real property actions or real property proceedings.

In short, if you hold a mortgage and the borrower doesn't repay as agreed, you can take the property back. But you must follow the laws of your state . . . and it can be expensive and time consuming.

THE DOCUMENT

- Under ordinary circumstances, the loan is evidenced by either a promissory note or a bond, or a trust deed and note with numerous conditions (usually called covenants) that the borrower accepts to receive the money.

- Sometimes, money does not actually change hands. This typically takes place when a seller gives what is called a "purchase money mortgage," or "takes back" paper from a borrower who either lacks the ability to obtain credit elsewhere, or finds a seller who has made a financial decision to become the "bank" in the transaction. In other words, the borrower purchases the property based on the down payment and any additional sum required, together with a mortgage. The "PM Mortgages" generally are a point or two greater than those offered by financial institutions, except that when interest rates are very high (as they were in 1980–1981), the rates can be lower to help "sell" a deal.

Note: In some states, such as California, a lender cannot secure a deficiency judgment (a personal judgment against the borrower) when sale of the property does not satisfy the loan amount, if the property is foreclosed through a trust deed sale. In other states, a deficiency judgment is widely available on commercial property transactions, but difficult to obtain on residential properties. (This is because most banks are required to appraise the property and cannot make the loan in the first place for more than the appraisal price and, typically, must make it for anywhere from 90 percent or less of the appraisal.)

Typically, at the time the lender agrees to advance funds, and the borrower agrees to pledge the real property as collateral, a title report or title search is ordered by the "mortgagee," or the person or entity lending the money. The purpose of the title report is to insure that no one else has a claim to, or on the property before the lender. (Title insurance is also available to second mortgage holders, which insures that other than the first mortgage, no one has greater priority than the second mortgagee to the property's security interest.)

Every state has a recording statute. This governs the manner in which deeds, mortgages, deeds of trust, and other liens may be recorded relative to real property in the office of the County Clerk, Register, or other similar official. The statutes (and their effect) differ in each state. Most typically, a statute provides that once recorded, the instrument, or lien, or other encumbrance has priority—or preference—against instruments that are subsequently recorded. In other words, once you as a lender record the mortgage, it comes before other most other liens recorded afterward. It has no priority with respect to instruments recorded before it.

 Thus if a judgment were entered against somebody on January 1, *but not recorded,* and the property owners were to place a mortgage on their house on January 5, which was promptly recorded, and the judgment was then recorded on January 10—even though the judgment was awarded first, it would not have priority over the mortgage, which was recorded first. If the mortgage was foreclosed, the judgment could not be collected out of the real property proceeds until after the mortgagee was paid in full.

FORECLOSURE PROCEDURES

The time that a foreclosure procedure takes, from start to finish, varies widely. In some states, foreclosure proceedings can take between three and four months, typically where a deed of trust is used, and what is called "foreclosure by advertisement" is employed. In other states, where judicial process is resorted to, it can last as long as a year and sometimes even longer because of the procedural steps that are required to remove someone of their property rights.

Conceptually, the Anglo-Saxon system of law places great emphasis on property rights and is reluctant to disturb them except under the most carefully controlled circumstances. Thus, a typical view that foreclosure is the vindication of a lender's legal right must be tempered with the knowledge that courts strictly construe the statute *against* the lender, and *in favor of* the borrower in a foreclosure action.

The reason: At the end, the borrower can lose his or her property in its entirety. If you hold a trust deed, the foreclosure procedure to follow can typically be given to you by a title insurance company or a real estate attorney. It is not difficult, but it does require precisely following time constraints and advertising when and where required. You do not need an attorney, but if you have not done it before, having an attorney at least spell out the procedure required in your state is advisable.

Chapter 17

How Do I Cure a Default on My Mortgage?

A default on a mortgage occurs when a material term contained in the mortgage, or the note that it secures, is not complied with. Sometimes this can be nonpayment, but other times it can be what seems to be an innocuous clause in the instrument—but proves not to be. Here are some reasons a lender may say you've defaulted on the mortgage:

- Failed to make timely monthly payments.
- Failed to keep the property in good repair.
- Rented out the property instead of living in it yourself. (Yes, some mortgage documents provide you must occupy the property yourself. This obviously is not applicable to commercial property. Take it seriously on residential properties, for while one of the authors questions the validity of the clause, the other would tell you it would be very expensive to be the leading case to challenge the contract that you voluntarily signed.)
- Materially damaged or changed the property. For example, began to tear down the house in anticipation of later building a new one, without the specific written consent of the lender.
- Failed to provide adequate insurance on the property.

WHAT ABOUT LATE PAYMENTS?

If the borrower has not been a good borrower and makes late payments almost every month, the lender will not be amused. However, unless the loan documents provides otherwise, merely making a late payment—within 15 days of the due date—doesn't give the right to call the loan, or to place it in default. Even if the payment is more than 15 days late, there is usually a financial penalty specified to which the lender can resort. Typically, if the monthly payment is not made within the 15-day grace period, the lender may assess a 5 percent of the payment penalty. However, if the borrower is consistently late, particularly several months late, the lender may eventually become frustrated and begin foreclosure proceedings.

WHAT'S THE LENDER'S PROCEDURE?

Nearly all promissory notes, and mortgages and other security agreements, provide that if an event of default occurs, the lender has the ability to declare a higher (the unpaid) balance of the unpaid note to be immediately due and owing. In other words, the lender will send you a notice that you are in default and will begin action to reclaim the property. As a practical matter, however, most lenders are unenthusiastic about doing this. Here's why: Banks that loan on mortgages, typically, don't own real estate. Likewise, the seller who took a purchase mortgage. Banks lend money; sellers want to sell, not be a lender.

HOW TO CURE YOUR DEFAULT

Here are some general steps to take if you've failed to make payment and the loan goes into default (the same holds true for technical violations of the terms and conditions of the mortgage or security agreement, and the underlying note):

- Call the lender and inquire if the bank will let you make late payments (if you're only one payment behind); that, if accepted, usually cures the default.
- If you're a couple of payments behind, find out whether the bank will allow you to make deferred payments until you've caught up.
- Check out your finances, see what you can afford, and then make a specific proposal to the bank to see whether you can preserve your ownership position by having them reduce or forgive some of the interest, if you begin making payments now. (Many lenders are willing to do this in a bad market where taking a property back can mean a substantial loss for them.)
- Be flexible, be willing to negotiate, and let the bank know that you'd prefer to renegotiate payment terms than go into foreclosure (see Chapter 17).

WHERE DO I START WHEN I RECEIVE
MY FIRST WARNING?

Many times, you'll receive a warning beforehand that you're in default. This is called a notice to cure, because it usually says that if you have not cured the defect within a short time period—usually 15 days or less—the entire unpaid principal balance will become due and owing.

There's a catch to this: Sometimes the financial institution wants your property! Perhaps it has gone up in value and the lender would rather have the real estate than the loan. Other times, they may want the cash they loaned you back. Either way, they may be trying to squeeze you, and force you to take them out of the loan. If this is the case, they can serve such a notice and then try to follow through. You, however, can seek a temporary restraining order or preliminary injunction from a court of competent jurisdiction; if the acceleration is unjustified, a court can stop it. Always be responsive to an acceleration notice; don't ignore it.

 If you apply for judicial relief, be certain that you do it before acceleration, since some courts take the view that they cannot revive a mortgage that has been accelerated, but can prevent someone from calling the mortgage and making it immediately due. Many defaults are easily curable within the statutory time period. Say, for example, that your homeowner's insurance policy is changed from one company to another, and you've forgotten to name the mortgagee as a loss payee. That technically violates the mortgage and could trigger an event of default. What happens as a practical matter in a case like that, however, is that the notice calling for termination is met by return mail with a copy of the insurance declaration page, naming the mortgagee a loss payee.

IS IT SERIOUS?

Because of the possibility that the loan will become due, it's important to take communication of default from the lender seriously, and to respond to the notice. If a "cure" to the problem is at hand, call it to the lender's attention by telephone (following up with a fax or hand-delivered letter). Although there are exceptions, most lenders will prefer not to call a default or even to battle for a higher rate of interest, performance issues, or for different payment terms. But they have to have someone to talk to—you. If you don't communicate, a lender will always assume the worst.

 Above all, negotiate with the lender—but be realistic with your expectations. At a certain point in time, even a bank would rather take their chances with a foreclosure than lose a lot of money renegotiating terms. Workouts by banks happen all the time. Bad things happen to otherwise good loans, and the bank wants to try and salvage the loan, the credit relationship, and their balance sheet. There's nothing the matter with that. In sum, when you're on the verge of default, don't give up the ship. Tough it out, and the ocean that you sail into could well have calm waters.

Chapter 18

How Fast Can a Judicial Foreclosure Throw Me Out of My Home?

You haven't paid your mortgage because you're out of a job. The 15th of the month comes, and goes, without your payment being made. You've paid for years on a regular basis—because you have this fear that the sheriff will be there to throw you out on the 16th day. Relax. Your troubles aren't over, but a foreclosure typically takes time, and considerable effort. When a lender—usually a bank—tries to take your property away from you, the law protects you, and your property, for as long as possible. Although the law of foreclosure differs state by state, in general, two types of foreclosure are utilized, depending on what part of the country you are in.

"Foreclosure by advertisement" is typically used when the mortgage instrument is a trust deed and is more common in the western part of the United States (see Chapters 16 and 21). "Judicial foreclosure" is used when the debt instrument is a mortgage and is more commonly used in the eastern part of the country.

JUDICIAL FORECLOSURE

Here's the general procedure in states that utilize the judicial process. A foreclosure is typically commenced by a letter sent to the mortgagor (you) demanding cure (typically for nonpayment). At the same time, the letter usually contains a notice of acceleration (making the entire loan and not just the delinquent payment(s), immediately due) if payment is not made by a particular day. An alternative approach is for a second letter to acknowledge that the time to cure has expired, and the full amount of the debt has been accelerated, and that the lender will no longer accept reinstatement of the mortgage, but instead will only accept payment of the entire indebtedness.

Simultaneously with either of these two approaches, a title company is typically notified by the lender, sometimes by telephone, sometimes by mail (sometimes both) and asked to perform what is known as a "foreclosure search." This checks out the title, and the title company will certify to the lender's attorney the necessary parties who must be joined in a foreclosure proceeding to protect the lender's interests. (You might have a third, fourth, or even higher mortgage in addition to the one that is being foreclosed. The lender may need to take action on those to protect his or her interests.) Once the title search has been received, a lender's attorney prepares a summons, complaint, and notice of pendency of action, sometimes referred to as a *lis pendens.* The summons is a piece of paper that acts to require its named recipient (you) to respond within a certain time frame, or to lose the right to address the court on the merits of the complaint. A complaint is just what it sounds like, and constitutes (sometimes in stilted, archaic form) the substance of what relief the mortgagee seeks.

The Judicial Complaint

- Recites who the parties are.
- Explains their status.
- Tells the court why it has jurisdiction (typically because it is real property situated within the court's jurisdiction).
- Explains the venue, or court chosen, and then goes on to recite a junior lienor interests that it wishes to foreclose against.
- Also recites the factual basis of the security agreement that allows it to commence the foreclosure proceedings in the first place.

The notice of pendency of action, or *lis pendens,* once filed, is intended to be notice to the world that a claim has been made that affects the right, title to, or interest in real property. It is designed to let a purchaser know that the property is being foreclosed against, and hence that if it is purchased from its current owners, it is done at the peril of the buyer.

DELIVERING THE COMPLAINT

Once the complaint and its allegations are verified by the lender, a process server is sent out to serve the complaint. This is tricky business, and it is one of the ways foreclosures can be derailed, delayed, or subsequently set aside as being defective.

- The lender need not physically hand you the complaint, but it is essential for the lender to give notice that is reasonably calculated to reach you. Sometimes this can mean in-hand service; other times substituted service is permitted (on a spouse, an office coworker, or other obscure means that are set forth by statute in your state).

- Personal delivery to you may be necessary by the lender, if there is a possibility that a "deficiency judgment" may arise. (A deficiency judgment hits you up for more money personally because the house won't sell for enough to pay off the mortgage.) Many courts are loath to grant a deficiency judgment if someone has not been personally served, and had actual notice that this became an object of the proceeding, as opposed to mere foreclosure of a parcel of land. The lender also serves any junior lenders you may have on the property (other lenders who hold mortgages).

Helpful Hint You can't avoid service—or prevent the foreclosure action from proceeding—by not "taking" the papers from the legal process from the process server or the sheriff. The law will simply presume that as long as the papers were in your general vicinity, you've received them.

- When a corporation is involved, the lender can serve the Secretary of State, or the State Bureau of Corporations, since it leaves no doubt that there is good service—even if you ultimately never have any actual notice at all. The reason for this is that corporations are artificial creatures, created by statute, and the same statute that creates them directs how they may be served.

- If you cannot be found, the process is delayed because in the failure to obtain service, there is no jurisdiction, and the interest cannot be foreclosed.

- If you cannot be found, the court can work around it. Procedures to deal with this often call for the court to fashion a means of obtaining service, sometimes by publishing notice in a newspaper. Once service is complete, you typically have approximately a month to put in an answer or a response. If you are on the receiving end of a foreclosure summons and complaint, and if you really have no defense, it makes little sense to put in an answer. All that it does is make needless expense for your adversary and sets up the possibility that the lender will offer you no cooperation at all should there be proceeds left over after the underlying mortgage is satisfied. In fact, a Notice of Appearance and Waiver in Foreclosure is typically used.

 If you're a borrower being foreclosed, you can sometimes bargain with a lender to offer you some consideration—payment—to not contest the foreclosure proceeding. Sometimes, you can even bargain for time to continue to reside at the premises (see Chapter 20). When service is complete and the time to answer has expired, the next step usually is to ask the court for appointment of a referee to compute. A referee is typically a lawyer, or retired judge, whose job it is to determine (officially) the amount due on the mortgage, whether the mortgaged parcel should be sold as a whole, or as multiple parcels, and (ultimately) will conduct the sale on the courthouse steps. Before the referee to compute can be appointed, any defenses that may exist with respect to the foreclosure action must be dealt with. This will typically involve both affirmative defenses and counterclaims (if a junior lender is involved).

CONCLUSION OF FORECLOSURE

If a foreclosure is contested, a lender will seek summary relief from the court, usually by way of a motion or application to the court to receive a judgment of foreclosure and sale. This request, called a motion for summary judgment, asks for expeditious handling of the request. Unless there is a real issue of fact—such as the bank never lent you the money, the note isn't secured properly by the mortgage, or something similar—that motion usually will be granted.

The next step in the process is for the lender to obtain the judgment of foreclosure and sale, and again a judge is involved. The matter is typically submitted, and after some period of time (which can range from a day to several weeks) a judgment is entered and a certain sum, and a referee (typically the same person who computed previously) is designated to sell your home on the courthouse steps. There is usually a requirement that the sale be published—some states require it be published for a period of four weeks prior to the sale; the court designates the newspaper in which the advertisement will appear.

Although it is highly unlikely that you will receive actual notice in this fashion, it doesn't matter. The courts have ruled that this procedure can be followed. Typically, the referee works with the lender's attorney and sets a sale date, anywhere between six to eight weeks in the future. This allows for the requisite advertisement to be placed. Come the day of the sale, in many counties it actually does take place on the courthouse steps; in others it is in the rotunda, and in at least one it is in a sales room. There many bidders in attendance—you can be one of them, if you like, so long as you can make the required payment.

This usually includes 10 percent down payment by cash at the sale, and the balance within 30 days of closing—all cash, no mortgage or financing allowed. If no one bids, the mortgage holder (usually the bank or funding company) becomes the owner by way of a referee's deed. If there are bidders, the bank can bid up to the amount of the mortgage, plus accrued interest and costs (the amount of the judgment) without actually having to advance any cash.

Bidding is held, your home is sold and, shortly thereafter, the sheriff will come to remove you, if you haven't already left. (This part of the process, called eviction, takes a while, also; but at the end of the day, the lender gets possession of the premises.) The entire process can take anywhere from a few months to a year or longer.

THINGS TO DO

When a foreclosure proceeding is initiated against you, do not despair. Here are some of the things that you can do:

Helpful Hint   Call up your lender and see if they are interested in negotiating. Lenders typically do not want to own your property; they want to have money that they can lend again.

Helpful Hint   Contact a junior lender with a subordinated lien and inquire whether it would be willing to buy out your position to protect its rights. Sometimes, this is the only remedy that you have, but will give you some capital or return on your investment.

Helpful Hint   Read the complaint, and the summons carefully, see if there are any errors. If there are errors, you may be able to delay the proceedings substantially. Typically, you do this by filing an answer to the complaint, and filing with the court all of the technical objections, and other objections, that you may have.

Helpful Hint   One thing is essential to remember: If you receive a demand letter stating that a foreclosure proceeding will be forthcoming, and that payment in full is required, you should take it seriously.

Chapter 19

How Can I Defend against Losing My Property through Foreclosure?

If gutter fighting is your forte, then defending against a mortgage foreclosure action will make you feel right at home. Even so, it won't be a picnic fighting to keep your home. Foreclosure actions typically begin with a demand by the lender that you (the mortgagor) comply with some term or condition of the mortgage. Usually—but not always—it calls for payment to be made to the lender (see Chapter 16). Sometimes that payment is simply a monthly payment gone awry; after there has been a serious default with the payment, typically the unpaid amount of the mortgage is sought, together with interest and lender's legal fees, if any.

You could be foreclosed on even if you are making your payments. Mortgages contain covenants and conditions, and a reluctant lender (mortgagee) can sometimes call a loan due based on a violation of those covenants—even if the underlying mortgage payment is being regularly, and systematically made in accordance with the mortgage note or bond. Typically, this occurs when the lender is insecure about the loan for some reason (such as you've let the property go to pot, or building violations have been imposed). With some degree of success, nearly every mortgage foreclosure action can be substantially delayed, principally because the law is so reluctant to allow itself to be used for the purpose of taking away real property from an owner (albeit one who is really only a partner with the financing party, who now isn't getting paid).

DEFENSES

Borrowers can use a litany of affirmative defenses in attempting to halt a foreclosure proceeding in its tracks. You can claim:

- Partial payment has been made, that lender hasn't credited (you) borrower for. If the lender (mortgagee) accepts partial payment, the foreclosure procedure may terminate and the lender must go back to the beginning to institute it again.

- Usury, meaning that the lender charged too much interest, in violation of state or federal statutes.
- Fraud.
- Duress.
- Illegality.
- Unconscionable conduct.
- Misrepresentation.

If you can prove these defenses, the mortgagee is likely to not only lose the ability to foreclose the mortgage, but may also no longer have the ability to make you repay the underlying loan. There are also some procedural or technical defenses that can have the effect of making the lender's counsel go back to the beginning and start the foreclosure process again—usually much to their chagrin. These include:

- A successful claim that process was defectively served.
- Failure to properly name all parties and to properly serve each of them.
- Statute of limitations (the foreclosure was begun too late).
- Laches (the lender slept on his rights while allowing you to take actions to your detriment).
- Estoppel (the actions of the lender preclude recovery). Sometimes, you can put in an affirmative defense simply to buy time. It can be a useful negotiating tool, particularly if your circumstances are that you simply need a little bit of time to get your financial affairs in order.

DO I HAVE ANY LEVERAGE WITH THE LENDER?

Your leverage in the context of renegotiating is:

- The lender will have to foreclose if terms cannot be reached with you. That will take time (perhaps a year) and money (cash out of pocket). By negotiating and reaching agreement, the terms are solidified and agreed to, now.

- If you really don't like the results, you can trap the lender into defending an expensive bankruptcy proceeding—no one's idea of fun. In one residential foreclosure of a loan of more than $1 million that wound up in the bankruptcy court to resolve disputes between competing mortgagees, the application for counsel fees exceeded $100,000 from all attorneys involved (*In re Rundlett,* 136 B.R. 376 (S.D.N.Y. 1992)).

- A technical look at the note and documents securing the loan may very well disclose technical violations of the Fair Credit Reporting Act, Truth in Lending Act, and the Fair Debt Collection Practices Act, leaving the lender potentially liable for legal and attorney's fees.

Helpful Hint   Some jurisdictions require that an entire controversy be litigated in one action, and that all counterclaims that are available be raised. So if a defense is required and there is a truth-in-lending issue, or some other technical one, be sure that you consider raising these issues.

- A renegotiated loan is still an active and a good loan; the lender doesn't have to fall back on reserves to fix the problem.

- If you reach agreement, the loan won't be considered nonperforming—a clear benefit to the bank.

- It's easier to give up some portion of the interest than it is to lose the entire loan, which becomes a writeoff, and something that has to be justified to federal regulators. Of course, merely stating a defense doesn't prove your defense. Most courts will allow you to raise that issue, but eventually it becomes a question of proof. At that time, you will need to have hard evidence—proof—of the claim that you are making in the attempt to defeat the mortgagee's interest. There are two types of delay in a foreclosure action: the first is technical, the other is more substantive. Each can be equally effective in delaying the foreclosure proceeding, but also in substantially increasing the cost of the legal action.

 Any time that you exercise an affirmative defense, you need to consider that the work that you put the other side through ultimately is at your expense—especially if you are trying to reinstate the mortgage. If you ask the lender to restore the mortgage, you will most likely be liable for all the lender's attorney's fees involved in the foreclosure.

DEFEND A FORECLOSURE YOURSELF?

In the event that you find your mortgage being foreclosed, it is essential that you take prompt action. You must answer the complaint; you can't ignore it! You can decide whether or not to proceed yourself or let an attorney represent you as the events go on. Sometimes, defending yourself can work out very well because courts make every effort to assist litigants without counsel, especially where their home is at stake. If you wish to raise a defense, however, it will be necessary to go to court, file the appropriate documents, and make appearances. If you have a trust deed, chances are the lender is avoiding court action and instead is foreclosing by advertisement (see Chapters 16, 18, and 19). You will need to go to court to stop the action. If it is judicial foreclosure, the court is already involved. Either way, unless you are experienced in these matters, you will probably be well served by legal representation, at least the first time it happens.

OTHER TACTICS

- If you are sure you're going to lose your property in any event (you have no hope of making the payments), you can attempt to give a deed to the property to the lender in lieu of foreclosure. A "deed in lieu of foreclosure" (see also the next chapter) helps save your credit somewhat. (Future lenders recognize it for what it is, but at least it's a step better than foreclosure; many credit requests, however, will ask if you have ever had a property foreclosed on, or offered a deed in lieu of foreclosure.) Lenders, however, do not have to accept the deed. Therefore, you may need to negotiate with them. Sometimes presenting the alternatives, either accept the property now, in good condition, or go through foreclosure and get it months later in dubious condition, can be a powerful motivator to get the lender to accept a "deed in lieu."
- As a last-ditch method of fighting against foreclosure, you can always file for bankruptcy reorganization. That throws a real curve at lenders, at least initially. The mere act of filing under Chapter 7 (liquidation), Chapter 11 (reorganization), or Chapter 13 (wage earner's plan) automatically stays any legal proceeding. It means that the lenders are stopped in their tracks, cold. Of course, lenders have the ability to circumvent the automatic stay by making a motion to the bankruptcy court seeking relief from the automatic stay. But that, too, is time consuming and can add months to the process.

You need to analyze what your goal is—delay so that you can refinance, or delay so that you can simply stay as long as possible—and negotiate with the lender for your best deal (either payment to have you leave, or forgiving some portion of the debt).

 Remember, most lenders don't really want to own your property or take it back. They almost always want to make a deal with you. Sometimes, it can be as easy as proposing that payments be stretched out to give you some relief. Other times, it may involve canceling some interest or debt. Once the foreclosure proceeding has begun, it is important for you to be organized. Create a file and keep every sheet of paper that is generated. You'll need it—either to help defend, or to provide information to your lawyer as he or she commences a defense. Fasten related papers together and file chronologically. It will be much easier, later on, when you need a document or a reference point. Don't be intimidated by lenders. They don't want to take your property any more than you want to give it up. Negotiate!

Chapter 20

Deed in Lieu of Foreclosure—
Pros and Cons

In the silent movies, the villainous banker was always foreclosing on the ranch by thrusting a paper boldly labeled "deed" into the face of the fair maiden, and asking her to sign over the property to him. What he was asking for was a deed in lieu of foreclosure in which the mortgagor (or the owner and borrower on the land) voluntarily tenders title to the lender to avoid a foreclosure lawsuit. Deeds in lieu of foreclosure are relatively well known, but are rarely used properly to the advantage of the property owner who is in default of the mortgage, usually for nonpayment rather than some technical violation.

ADVANTAGES TO THE BORROWER

Think about it: You've signed a mortgage, promising to pay, and you can't. You're indebted to your lender. And the lender then lets you out of the mortgage. Indeed, in some cases the lender even *pays you* to get out of the transaction—forgiving your debt in the process, and not obtaining a deficiency judgment. Would you jump at the chance?

ADVANTAGES TO LENDER OF A DEED IN LIEU

A deed in lieu of foreclosure tendered by the owner of the parcel saves the lender a great deal of expense and time—often tens of thousands of dollars in hard cash and as much as a year or more before the lender obtains possession, and then additional time to sell or resell to regain the money lost on the mortgage. The following list shows the hypothetical real cost to the lender on a mortgage of, say, $150,000 on a 10 percent mortgage (assuming routine foreclosure without significant opposition):

- One year's lost interest, $15,000.
- Prospective attorney's fees, $1,500.
- Taxes, $3,000.
- Subsequent maintenance by lender, $5,000.
- Eviction process, $1,500.
- Ability to relend $3,000 in principal, and $300 in interest, totals $3,300.
- Foreclosure search, $300.
- Office time devoted to bad loan, $1,000.
- Disbursements for foreclosure legal process, excluding attorney's fees, $3,500.

There are other intangible expenses, and some tangible ones, but these alone total as much as $40,000, some of it cash out of pocket, some of it lost opportunity. If you (the borrower) were to decide in the midst of the process to file for bankruptcy, that would further tie up the land and the mortgage in the legal system, and could result in an additional $3,500 to $5,000 in legal fees. If, as a businessperson, you were told that you could buy your way out of a $40,000 loss for, say, $5,000—and the costs that you would incur are a guaranteed savings, it might make good economic sense to undertake the transaction. That is the lender's motivation to accept a deed in lieu.

Does it still make sense for the lender to accept a deed in lieu if the estimated costs are much less, say, $10,000? Perhaps it does—especially if the borrower indicates he or she is going to offer an especially hard time in the foreclosure process.

THE NEGOTIATIONS

For this all to happen will take some negotiation, since a lender isn't voluntarily going to part with money, and a borrower doesn't start with a great deal of strength—unless they have experience doing this type of transaction. That probably means that you'll have to secure assistance.

A lawyer can help. You can also use a company that specializes in helping debtors restructure and get a fresh start. They can provide some of the answers, and a lot of assistance in starting the negotiating process.

DOWNSIDES

Is there a downside to all this? Of course there is, and that's one of the reasons that you may want to contemplate alternatives to a deed in lieu of foreclosure, and instead contemplate selling the premises to a lender at a substantially reduced price, subject to the mortgage.

 There can be a significant tax consequence to giving a deed in lieu of foreclosure, especially if your indebtedness to the lender is canceled. The Internal Revenue Code provides that forgiveness of indebtedness constitutes income. So if you're not very careful, you can have an unintended income tax consequence.

 If you sell to your lender (not really a deed in lieu of foreclosure) at a loss—perhaps for a sum exceeding the mortgage, but less than your original purchase price plus all capital improvements—there probably isn't a tax loss, and any payout that you retain you might be able to keep tax free.

 If you negotiate for a deed in lieu or equivalent, remember to calculate the cost of the transfer tax on the property, and who will bear that cost. The transfer tax can be substantial—in some jurisdictions, as much as 2 percent of the purchase price—so that can make a difference. (From our perspective, it simply ought to be how much the lender has to pay; from their perspective, how little.)

Chapter 21

Trust Deed Foreclosures
(by Advertisement)

Foreclosure by advertisement (used with a trust deed) is permitted by statute in all states, though it is rarely used in the eastern United States. It is fast, efficient, and in general increasingly preferred by both lenders and borrowers.

Currently, foreclosure by advertisement has widespread frequency and use in 24 states: Alabama, Alaska, Arizona, California, Colorado, Georgia, Hawaii, Idaho, Michigan, Minnesota, Mississippi, Missouri, Montana, Nevada, New Hampshire, North Carolina, Oregon, Rhode Island, Tennessee, Texas, Utah, Virginia, Washington, and West Virginia. Except for Connecticut and Vermont (which have a peculiar statute), the rest typically foreclose through the courts.

Foreclosure by advertisement is usually the case if you have a trust deed (instead of mortgage). In general, foreclosure by advertisement is faster and far easier than judicial foreclosure. (The lender usually can also opt to do a judicial foreclosure; however, the only reason a lender would likely choose to go this route is if the property isn't likely to bring enough money in a sale to cover the mortgage and foreclosure costs. Judicially, the lender may be able to obtain a deficiency judgment against you, personally. The lender cannot obtain a deficiency judgment when foreclosing through advertisement, since there is no judgment per se.)

PROCEDURE

The procedure moves swiftly. However, there are several periods during which you, the borrower, may redeem the property, first by paying up all current back payments, costs, and penalties and finally by paying back in full the entire amount of the mortgage plus costs and penalties. Eventually, the property is sold "on the courthouse steps" to the highest bidder and is lost forever to you.

This type of foreclosure can be fast. The entire procedure, for example, can only take four months or so in California. If you are a borrower who wants to redeem your property once foreclosure by advertisement has begun, check with your state's Department of Real Estate to determine the exact redemption periods and requirements. Then, be sure to redeem the mortgage before they expire.

If you pay up, no lawyer is required, although you want to have someone knowledgeable check the paperwork. Advertising is the key to this type of foreclosure. An advertisement is placed in a general circulation newspaper, usually designated by a court, giving notice to all appropriate creditors, and junior lienors of the attempt that will be made to cut off their rights. (If the notice is defective in any way, the general rule is that the foreclosure by advertisement is ineffective.) There are specific time parameters for publication (e.g., once a week for 12 weeks), and there are posting requirements at specific courthouses (this must also be delivered to the county clerk, and a copy served upon the mortgagor) as well as other requirements that are quite capable of being reduced to a chart. In the final analysis, perhaps the single largest reason why foreclosure by advertisement is not utilized in New York, and in some other states, is that title companies have found that an appreciable risk goes into using this medium, and hence are reluctant to give the necessary title insurance that should devolve as part of the ownership. On the other hand, foreclosure by advertisement, or a "power of sale" foreclosure, is widely used in both western and southern states.

For that reason, the argument commonly heard in the Eastern states that the notice provisions are constitutionally infirm and should be firmly rejected appears tenuous at best. (Something cannot be inappropriate in New York but perfectly appropriate in California, when what is involved is the identical right, title, and interest to real property.)

Suffice it to say that litigation involving foreclosure by advertisement in states that favor judicial foreclosure probably favors the borrower; hence, the resort to the courts. Where a deed of trust or a trust deed is utilized (as is common in a power-of-sale state), the borrower is typically asked to waive the right to a court proceeding in the event of a default.

Helpful Hint Typically, notice periods are provided, and minimum notice periods are specified to prevent an abuse or unfair taking of property. Find out the notice periods for your state and put them on a calendar or chart. If you want to defend against foreclosure, do so within the parameters of the notice period. Failure to take timely action could cost you your home!

In Vermont, there similarly is no foreclosure sale. If a mortgagor fails to redeem the property during the period of redemption, the title vests absolutely in the mortgagee.

The nonjudicial power of sale foreclosure in California is set forth in California Civil Code 2924. In that state, the trustee initiates the nonjudicial foreclosure at the request of the beneficiary of the trust (the lender) if a default is noted, and a reinstatement period is then commenced (90 days). If a default is not cured, the trustee commences publication for 21 days. The property owner or junior lienor has a period prior to the trustee sale to redeem. After the sale takes place, a trustee's deed is prepared, signed, and recorded. California has no right of redemption after a trustee sale made pursuant to foreclosure by advertisement, except to the extent that federal statute may permit the government to redeem if a tax lien is involved. The difference between the California approach and that of, say, Missouri (where both judicial and nonjudicial methods are utilized), is that in Missouri, if the mortgagor gives written notice of intent to redeem either at the sale or within 10 days prior, the mortgagor then has a year to redeem.

STRICT FORECLOSURE

There is also a "strict foreclosure" proceeding utilized in Connecticut and Vermont. Each is similar and differs from that used in the 48 other states and the District of Columbia. In Connecticut, homeowners are given the first "law date" by which they must pay off the foreclosing mortgage holder or lose their interest in the property. The most junior lien holder is then given a second law date to do the same. The third law date is given to the second most junior lien holder, and so on. After all the lien holders have failed to pay off the foreclosing mortgage, title vests absolutely in the foreclosing mortgage holder.

 From a lender's perspective, foreclosure can prove to be both a bane, and an opportunity. For the astute investor, it can constitute a means to acquire property inexpensively (at the sale).

 It can also constitute a means by which a property can be freed from liens, and can also constitute a methodology of severing a bad debtor-creditor relationship.

Finally, from a lender's perspective, the threat of losing the parcel is frequently sufficient to chasten even the most difficult of borrowers, such as the one who needs to be reminded each month that the mortgage obligation has a top priority.

 From a borrower's perspective, foreclosure is anything from an irritant (if it's only short lived and the loan reinstated) to a full disaster. The best advice here, is to act promptly and communicate with the lender (see also Chapter 17).

Chapter 22

How Do I Pick the Right Lawyer to Foreclose on a Mortgage That I Hold?

Is this you? You took back a purchase money mortgage when you sold your house. You believed you would receive a high interest rate and then, after a specific period of time, your capital would be returned. Only the buyer hasn't made the payments as contemplated. Now you need to foreclose to get your property back.

Where do you turn? What do you do?

Most individuals who need to foreclose on a mortgage are not traditional private lenders with vast resources. Usually, they are average citizens who are short on both cash and knowledge. So, they want to secure the services of a lawyer at a minimum of expense; but which lawyer?

When John F. Kennedy became president, one of his first appointments was his brother, Robert, to become attorney general. "He's never practiced law," JFK is purported to have said, "so I thought I would give him some on-the-job training." The law of foreclosure is arcane and steeped with minefields that the unwary can trigger. Significant time delays can be stretched into many months—and even years—if a wrong move is made. While a general practitioner can learn the necessary skills on the job, as Robert F. Kennedy did, there is little doubt that this will be a time-consuming exercise. It will inevitably delay the day of reckoning for the mortgagor and might end up costing you more money.

CAN YOU DO IT YOURSELF?

Perhaps, if it's nothing more than a trust deed, commonly used as a mortgage instrument in most of the country. More likely, if you've gone through it a couple of times before with an attorney's help. If it is judicial foreclosure (going to court), less likely. Either way there are a number of forms that assist the petitioner in foreclosure—it

100

is a paper-heavy proceeding. But even with these, the amount of time involved can be substantial, and someone who does not specialize in foreclosures, or do many of them, has little economy of scale. Indeed, at the end of a typical foreclosure (uncontested judicial proceeding), plaintiff or plaintiff's counsel has a one-inch-thick file of paperwork. On the bright side of foreclosure proceedings, in many states, the courts recognize that it is time consuming and expensive, and that a substantial legal right has been prejudiced by the failure to pay the mortgage. In other words, the court will likely be friendly to you.

SELECTING A LAWYER

Because of the complexity of foreclosure proceedings, a "plaintiff's foreclosure bar" has developed. Participants are attorneys who are familiar with this area of law; some even limit their practice to referrals from this bar only. They may advertise in the yellow pages of the phone book. Or check with your local county or city bar association, which can probably supply you with the names and telephone numbers of several local practitioners who are skilled in the field—and who will answer your initial questions at no charge. Finally, you may be able to obtain their names from a title insurance company. If you do proceed with a foreclosure, insist on interviewing the lawyer, first. Here's a checklist of questions to ask. A satisfactory answer on almost all of them means that the lawyer is probably experienced enough to properly handle your foreclosure claim in timely fashion:

- How many foreclosures has the lawyer has handled in the past year, and how many over his or her career?
- What is the shortest time that the lawyer ever required to handle a foreclosure from commencement to sale of the parcel?
- What is the longest time that the lawyer required for any foreclosure proceeding?
- Does the lawyer handle work personally, assign it to an associate, or ask another firm or lawyer to handle it "of counsel"?
- Does the lawyer perform foreclosure work for a fixed fee or on an hourly basis?
- What total disbursements can you reasonably expect to pay in the course of a foreclosure that proceeds to sale?

- Are there additional charges (if a fixed fee is agreed on) for a motion for summary judgment if necessary?

There are no right or wrong answers to these questions, but if the person answering them isn't comfortable—or if you don't like the answers, you may want to think about asking someone else. It is also important to remember that in any foreclosure proceeding, your aim as a mortgagee is not retribution, or revenge. It's to get paid the money that you are owed on the mortgage. Selecting an attorney who shares that goal will help you realize it.

 Foreclosure is one of the few causes of legal action that, when prosecuted, entitles you (the mortgagee) to substantial court costs. In a contested foreclosure proceeding, the amount you may receive, likely will not begin to approach the real cost of the litigation, but in an uncontested foreclosure proceeding, particularly if there is a reduction, it can go a long way toward compensating for a lawyer and payment of all charges incurred. More importantly, if the foreclosure proceeding terminates favorably, you as lender can usually demand, as a condition of resolution, that all of your attorney's fees be paid by the party being foreclosed. In 1996, typical expenses of a judicial foreclosure proceeding in New York (cash out of pocket), and not counting the attorney's fees, were as follows: foreclosure search (title company), $300; purchase of index number, $170; purchase of request for judicial intervention (apply for referee), $80; referee's report, $50; fee for referee selling parcel, $200; service of process, $145 for defendant, for foreclosure, minimum of five defendants, $225; advertisement in publication, $500 through $1,600 (once a week for four weeks). The out-of-pocket cost usually exceeds $2,000.

 If there are only a couple of thousand dollars left on the mortgage, it may not pay to bring on a foreclosure proceeding at all, but be more practical to wait the borrower out. When the borrower sells the parcel, the mortgage constitutes a lien that must be paid and discharged before a title company will insure it.

 Sometimes, you can bring a foreclosure in a court that has a lower monetary jurisdiction. Some of the out-of-pocket costs may be reduced that way because of lower filing fees.

Chapter 23

How Can I Renegotiate My Mortgage?

It's tough to make that monthly payment; in fact, it's impossible. What strength do I have if I want to renegotiate my mortgage, and what can I ask for? Your mortgage is secured by land and improvements on it; it may also be enforceable by your personal promise to pay. If you default, the mortgagee has the right to elect to bring a claim against you based on the mortgage, which is foreclosed upon, or the bond or note which may be sued on. But, like all legal promises, it can either be renegotiated, or extinguished under certain circumstances. Your strong point in dealing with any lender is that your mortgagee does not want to become a property owner. They are moneylenders. They make their profits based on money that they lend, not property that they own. Hence, there is a universal willingness to discuss, and even negotiate. Many times, this can actually include modification of terms.

Nearly every lender knows the horror of having to make a substantial expenditure of money for counsel fees, whether to foreclose, or to fight a matter in the bankruptcy court. Worse, some lenders are aware that they might be in technical violation of a number of federal statutes: Truth in Lending, Fair Credit Recording, and Fair Debt Collection practices, each of which can have substantial monetary and financial penalties. For this reason, there is frequently a strong motivation on the lender's part to negotiate with you and to assure that the loan remains booked as a positive asset.

WHAT YOU CAN ASK YOUR LENDER FOR

- Lower your monthly payment, and extend your term.
- Temporarily pay interest only, without reducing the mortgage for principal.
- Move from a fixed rate mortgage to a floating rate of interest.
- Make your mortgage into a hybrid if it exceeds $207,000; that is, place a first mortgage that meets Fannie Mae guidelines, and a

second mortgage that doesn't. The second mortgage can have a different schedule of payments than the first. One can be interest only for five years, while the other is amortizing.

- If the mortgage is truly customized, you may even get one month or so a year where the mortgages amortizes negatively, meaning you make no payment or a much reduced payment. What the lender is trying to avoid—and what you don't want to happen—is an event of default, which occurs when a material term of the mortgage, or the promissory notes, or any other underlying security agreement, or collateral agreement, is violated.

WHAT CAUSES DEFAULT?

Typical areas of default include the following:

- Failure to pay the principal payments, and the interest, when due.
- Failure to make a balloon payment when required.
- Failure to maintain property insurance.
- Failure to make a repair to the premises after the premises have been damaged.
- Failure to be responsive to, or with, a notice received from the lender requiring some actions to be taken.
- Executing an instrument of conveyance (such a deed) without securing the lender's approval. Commonly, this can happen when a husband and wife deed the property in the name of one spouse, only. It can also happen with a sale to a third, unreliable party.
- Failure to execute any "omitted" documents which should have been signed at the closing or misstatements on documents provided to the lender at the closing.
- Failure to disclose a significant change of circumstances between the time of loan application, and closing.
- Permitting a lien to remain on the premises for a period of time longer than it is permitted by the mortgage.
- Violating any material term of the mortgage agreement or any other agreement pledged on the promissory note.

The initial remedy that nearly every lender has when a significant condition has been violated (or when payment is not made as provided for in the promissory note) is to send a demand letter to the borrowers to remind them of their obligations, and, typically, to advise them that if the terms and conditions are not followed, the entire unpaid principal balance will be declared due and owing, immediately. Because most people do not have the ability to pay off a mortgage at once—indeed, that is why they borrow the money in the first place—this is warning of dire financial consequences that may result.

Helpful Hint In many jurisdictions, for a lender to accelerate the unpaid principal indebtedness requires a clear and unequivocal statement of the acceleration. Sometimes, it is insufficient to say, for example, that this "may be the consequences" so it is important to retain all papers and correspondence that you may receive from the lender relative to any purported accelerations.

Helpful Hint Rules vary from state to state—usually in direct proportion to the number of foreclosures—as to whether or not a court has the ability to reinstate a loan, once it is accelerated. If your state is one where reinstatement is not possible, it probably is permissible to obtain a "judicial stay" in the form of an order directing the status quo "continue" if there is a showing of special circumstances. Special circumstances might be that the violation is a largely technical one, not affecting the lender, who is using it as a pretext to get out of a bad loan. This typically happens when there is a wide disparity between current interest rates, and those of existing mortgage loan.

WHAT TO DO

If you find yourself in default, your initial best bet is not to avoid your responsibility but rather, to confront it head-on. If you do this, even if you can't afford to make an overdue payment, you will be 90 percent ahead of any of your contemporaries with similar problems. The reason for this is that most people try to avoid financial unpleasantness, rather than facing it.

Helpful Hint Because lenders want to continue being the bank, rather than the owner of the property, or a deficiency judgment, they are usually willing to work with you. Say, for example, you have lost your job—or have been ill and are drawing disability benefits. It's not enough to make the monthly payments, and to feed and clothe your spouse and children. The odds are strong that if you contact your lender, even after receiving a default notice, that they will renegotiate the terms of your loan temporarily—to give you time to pay.

Your negotiating strengths are greatest before the mortgage goes into default—when you can get the lender's attention to your good payment record, or some other attribute that will assist their decision in your favor. If there is a financial emergency, sometimes you can wait until you get a letter from the bank, and then simply respond; in many cases, the lender will waive the late interest penalties, and any other extra penalties associated.

 Getting penalties waived may take some fast talking, and isn't something that you can use regularly, but in an emergency, it can be a lifesaver. The lender almost always has the ability to waive penalties. Interest may be harder.

 It is in the bank's interest to keep the loan as a productive one. Until the loan goes into default, certain requirements have to be met, and it may prevent the bank from making other loans. Extending the term of the mortgage, or having interest only paid for a brief period, is better than losing the loan.

 It will take a while before the matter is referred to the foreclosure attorney, sometimes as long as eight months (under New York law, it will take another 9 to 12 months before the property could be foreclosed on successfully).

BEGIN NOW

- If you are in default, or close to it, think about how to negotiate with the bank.
- Call the bank, and attempt to negotiate; discuss your options, and see how creative the bank can be to help you.
- Keep the bank talking; do not avoid telephone calls, or ignore letters. Keep them talking, and you may even find that time, together with some luck (and perhaps an unexpected check) help cure the default.

Title to Real Property

Chapter 24

Do I Need Title Insurance When I Buy Real Estate?

Technically, you don't need title insurance any more than you need homeowner's insurance to offer peace of mind against a fire loss. But, just as no one with common sense would avoid fire insurance (actually, mortgage companies make this decision for you by demanding it), you should not avoid title insurance if given the opportunity. This unique form of protection that insures that you actually own your property, free and clear of impediments, is definitely worthwhile.

Title insurance is normally purchased at the same time as you buy your home. It insures you, the buyer (or in some cases the lender) against certain defects in the title such as that the seller really didn't own the property or that there were hidden mortgages or tax liens or that the boundaries weren't as specified.

ALTERNATIVES TO TITLE INSURANCE

There are alternatives to title insurance. You can go, on your own, to the local county clerk's office and visit the hall of records to see if the seller of the parcel has any liens or judgments that are recorded against it, or them. You can then check with the Secretary of State's office in your locale to ascertain whether or not there are any financing statements that have been filed under the Uniform Commercial Code or other state law. Then you can go to the local United States District Court to ascertain whether, in the bankruptcy court, there is a case pending in which the seller is named as a party. And, if your city has a building and fire department, you can check there for potential violations or for an improper certificate of occupancy.

You can hire a lawyer—or a title company—to do the work for you. An abstract company is sometimes used as a subcontractor to perform the work and assure quality control. You can do all of these things on your own to be certain you're getting clear title. Or, you can buy title insurance.

WHAT YOU GET WITH A TITLE INSURANCE POLICY

Here's what the typical title insurance policy examines and insures against:

- *Tax Description and Tax Search.* This verifies that the premises you are buying is identical to the tax lot, and informs you that the taxes are either paid or unpaid.

- *Building and Fire Department Searches.* If your municipality has a building and fire department, it will typically have its records searched for possible violations.

- *Street Report.* This ascertains whether there is legal (as opposed to practical or physical) access to the nearest public street from your residence. Without this, it is difficult to utilize your property.

- *Survey Check.* It makes certain that the metes and bound description matches; has the survey's descriptions read into the report (including any variations at the lot line); if the survey is more than six months old, typically will inspect to see that there have been no changes.

- *Bankruptcy Search.* This determines whether the seller has filed for bankruptcy.

- *Certificate of Occupancy Search.* It tells you exactly what the premises may be legally used for and allows you to compare the certificate's statement of number of rooms and floors with the visible physical plant.

- *Covenants and Restrictions That Run with the Land.* These are also reported. Some of them can be resolved by purchasing affirmative insurance from the title company.

- *Liens and Judgments.* The report will include any liens or judgments that have matured against the owners (and the land), including water and sewer charges in some municipalities. Title insurers are regulated by the state, as are virtually all types of insurance policies. They have the ability, after reporting a problem, of resolving it by offering affirmative insurance.

PROBLEMS YOU COULD AVOID

- Suppose that you are going to purchase a house in a rural area that is serviced by a dirt road. The title company finds out that this is a private, not a public road, and that a portion of it travels over the land of some third person. It is usually possible to obtain affirmative insurance that the owner (and new buyer) of the premises will be able to obtain access to the nearest legally opened street.

• Many older parcels in planned communities have covenants and restrictions that run with the land. For example, it may say that the owner cannot use the premises for stabling horses. If they are used—even years afterward—the lands could revert to the heirs of the original grantor of the deed with the restriction.

The title company will offer insurance that for so long as the premises are utilized as they are at the time of the transaction, there will be no reversion. Title insurance has considerable value even in areas that have been settled for a long time. On Long Island, New York, in the 1960s, for example, the area had been settled for more than 300 years yet a substantial claim was made that various Indian tribes had rights to land in Suffolk County, at the eastern tip of the Island. The claims were sustained, and the residents would have lost their homes—and substantial investments—had they not had the title insurance. The title insurance companies were less lucky, since they had been insuring the land for many years and had concluded that the ownership issue was an unlikely challenge. The cost of title insurance is regulated and not very expensive. Since most mortgage lenders require title insurance, anyway, the add-on cost for what is called the fee policy—for the homeowner—is a bonus. Remember that title insurance only gives you coverage up to a certain point in time for all events that took place during a previous point in time. A lien that is recorded afterward isn't insured.

 If you are buying a house that has an older survey, ask whether it is possible to have a survey inspection, instead of a new survey done; if that's not possible, see if the title company can get the surveyor to redate the old survey, a common practice. Either will cost you a lot less than a new survey.

 If your residence or building juts an inch or two onto your neighbor's land, ask for affirmative insurance from the title company that the premises will be entitled to remain that way for as long as the building shall stand. That's a bonus coverage you can rely on.

Remember that title insurance only gives you coverage up to a certain point in time for all events that took place during a previous point in time. A lien that is recorded afterward isn't insured against. Some jurisdictions allow the title company to sell you inflation coverage. It is relatively inexpensive and may be worthwhile considering.

If you are refinancing your property, ask the title company if they will give a reissue rate. It's lower than the regular rate, and will save you substantial premiums.

If you are a purchaser, ask the seller (or require it in the contract of sale) for a copy of the survey that seller used when he or she purchased. You can then ask the title company if they are willing to simply have a survey inspection of the premises and, instead of a new survey, they will use the old one (together with an affidavit of no change). The savings to you could be in the hundreds of dollars. Most title companies will do it—and Fannie Mae underwriting guidelines allow it—if the survey is less than 10 years old.

Chapter 25

Do I Need a Land Survey When I Buy Real Estate? Why?

George Washington was a surveyor. So was Lincoln. And anyone who has ever visited the old city of Boston will appreciate Ralph Waldo Emerson's claim in "Wealth": "We say the cows laid out Boston. Well, there are worse surveyors"! A survey is a recorded sketch of what your property looks like, drawn not by an artist, but by a professional land surveyor. The surveyor traces the legal metes and bounds description of the outside perimeter of a piece of property and shows how the land is actually laid out.

A survey print shows where the property is located relative to the nearest street or streets, and where various improvements are located on the parcel itself. A survey used in the purchase of real estate is typically either undertaken strictly for the purchase, or an older, earlier version is located as part of the search of various real estate and governmental records by paid professionals (typically a title or abstract company). They insure the results to guarantee that you are making a purchase free and clear of liens and encumbrances, and without a portion of your residence being on someone else's property, and vice versa. You may not be required to have a survey by a lender when you make a purchase, but you typically will want to locate one that has been done previously, even if it is just to satisfy yourself that your property looks as it is verbally described.

The survey should typically not be undertaken on your own, though there is no reason why you can't contact a licensed land surveyor to do it on your behalf. If you order title insurance, it will typically be ordered for you by a competent searcher (commonly called an Attorney's Search, though attorneys don't necessarily have to do it), by an abstract company (that issues a title insurance policy), by a title company itself, or by some combination.

A survey for the purchase of real estate can be as expansive, or as narrow, as you are willing to demand—or to pay for. Like many contracts, portions of it are negotiable—if you know what you need to ask for.

If you are acquiring a large parcel of many acres, it is improbable that it will be necessary or desirable to include anything more than the outlines of the perimeter, together with the general placement of any improvements such as a house, a barn, a swimming pool, or similar structures. For a smaller residential parcel, it is usually wise to include everything from the location of fences and hedges to the measured distance between your driveway and your neighbor's property. If you are making a purchase that involves bank financing, and it is a residence, the odds are that the bank will require that you have a survey that meets the underwriting guidelines of the Federal National Mortgage Association (Fannie Mae).

Even if you don't purchase with bank financing, a survey is useful because it presents an objective sketch of what you are buying, as opposed to the hype of a real estate agent, or the gratuitous comments of the seller. Note that certain modifications have been suggested. If you are able to utilize them, you may be able to save a considerable amount of money in your overall title costs which, after a bank's points, may be your highest closing expense.

WHY YOU WANT A SURVEY

- You need to know what the size and dimensions are of the parcel that you are acquiring. If the house is on a plot of land that is 60 feet by 100 feet, common in many metropolitan areas, you need to know that your entire residence and the accessories, such as garage, pool, and shed, is within your boundary. Typically, you do this with a survey of the land, which is guaranteed to the title company, and also guaranteed to you. (If you have a lawyer, it may be guaranteed to him or her, also.)

- Surveys are vital in bringing to light any encroachments by others on your property as well as unusual circumstances, such as easements. They are widely used in certificates and reports of title, and form the basis of nearly all title insurance policies, even if the description is less than precise (which is frequently the case for country land or large acreage parcels).

- To obtain financing, the survey, under Federal National Mortgage Association (FNMA—Fannie Mae) underwriting guidelines, must be less than three years old, and bear a raised seal or imprint of a licensed surveyor's name together with a date. The actual parcel involved must be shown running to all four corners (if the parcel is square) as marked by the surveyor.

UNDERTAKING A SURVEY

Surveys must be done by a licensed land surveyor, who will measure the metes and bounds of the legal description of your land (the outside perimeter that typically forms a square or rectangle), and be certain that the written document accurately reflects the facts that a physical inspection shows:

- The outside perimeter will typically show a course starting at a point or place called the *beginning,* which is both the place of commencement, and termination, of the written description of the parcel that you are purchasing.
- The course that the perimeter follows will be shown, including whether it is parallel or perpendicular to another course, or even to a nearby street. (You no doubt thought that high school geometry was a waste of time, and that there would be no reason or purpose for you ever to utilize that knowledge again. Guess again. You utilize it all the time in real estate surveys, particularly when you check the surveyor's angles to make certain that they are mathematically correct.)
- Often a "metes and bounds" description is given. This always starts with the words *"Beginning* at a point," and continues from that description to the rest of the courses. If a square parcel is involved it has four courses. It will start, typically, at a point, trace each of the courses, and then always return to "the point or place of *beginning.*"

YOU CAN FOLLOW THE SURVEY YOURSELF

There is no one more interested in the correctness of your purchase than you. If you are buying a country lot, or even an irregular city lot, you should check out the survey yourself. This is not particularly difficult. If the description is using degrees or an odd measurement, it is usually sketched out on a separate sheet of paper. Follow the description and then match it against the survey. Otherwise, you can merely tick off the distance on the survey itself, assuming that the metes and bounds description is properly contained on the survey. The survey sometimes will have more, owing adjacent lands or distances from a corner (but usually that will be referenced in the description, as in "distant 925 feet from the intersection of two corners"). In this manner, the actual legal description (metes and bounds) is used.

A survey will sometimes state on it the block and lot that is the subject of the survey, just as it will sometimes indicate a tax block and lot (if it differs from the regular block and lot), and under some circumstances the particular subdivision will be listed. Sometimes, the adjacent block and lots to the parcel will also be shown.

ERRORS IN SURVEYS

If for some reason the metes and bounds description does not trace out properly, first check and be certain that you have read the numbers correctly. Sometimes, however, a title report will transpose a number, or will not copy or read it correctly. If this is the case, you need to contact the title company immediately and advise them the survey and the legal description do not match. A corrected description is required before you can proceed further, and before you can close on a transaction to either buy, sell, or mortgage.

PROBLEMS THAT CAN ARISE
WITH SURVEY DESCRIPTIONS

- For country properties, it is not unusual for the metes and bounds description to decide that a course follows a line to a stump located in the middle of a swamp, moving thence toward the lands of a long-deceased farmer to a particular tree or other marker. So long as the marker is well known, it isn't a problem, and is insurable by most title companies. At a minimum, a photocopy of the survey should be retained in your file. The original survey should always be retained when possible.

- As noted, old surveys may not suffice. Surveys are extraordinarily expensive in some parts of the country.

 Sometimes, in lieu of obtaining a new survey, it is possible to obtain a redated survey from the surveyor, or his successor. Typically, this is done because of survey costs. If a lender tells you that a new survey is required, it is best to ascertain whether a survey update will be acceptable instead. To do this, a surveyor will go back to the site and measure and ascertain that the original survey is as stated; this is much less expensive than making an actual survey.

Another approach is to ask whether an older survey will be acceptable if a survey inspection is provided, made by the title company, and read into the Certificate and Report of Title. In no event is it appropriate to conclude a real estate transaction in the absence of a survey. The reason for this is that the survey is the key to virtually all other aspects of the transaction: the tax description (matched against the survey description), the concomitant tax search, the street report (if any), the survey reading, the survey inspection, and ultimately, the determination of what you are actually purchasing. The survey is the starting point, and the end point, of real estate purchases. You need to utilize it for your own benefit in making a property purchase.

Chapter 26

What Is a "Survey Reading" and "Survey Inspection" and Do I Need Them?

The principal purpose in utilizing a "survey reading" is to assure, first, that you have read the survey correctly, and that mortgageable portions of the parcel—as well as all portions of the fee and improvements—are within boundaries. A survey reading can be defined by its name: It is a "reading" of what the survey states (not what the survey fails to state). Typically, the concern of a survey reading is to locate objects that are found on the survey (e.g., a house, a garage, a fence, a driveway, an easement, or other such objects) and to state it in a straightforward manner. The survey is done by a surveyor; a survey reading could be prepared by any lawyer, or any other individual capable of literally reading the document and reciting what the document states or doesn't state.

A survey reading will describe the type of improvement on the land; for example, a two-story frame house located square in the middle of a parcel might be described as follows: "two and a half story frame house, located within bounds." Sometimes, a large item may be described as "not located" meaning that the surveyor has noted it, but has not listed its dimensions, or distance from the property line. A survey reading may refer to a party wall (a wall shared by two parties, going along the boundary line) and may show power wires that traverse the property. Most surveys will not make reference to mineral rights though in some circumstances it may be warranted to ask for either the redating of a survey (and hence, a new survey reading) or clarification of whether a covenant and restriction reserves such rights (see Chapter 28).

PROBLEMS THAT CAN ARISE FROM THE READING

- An apartment building in New York, or a large city, for example, may show on a survey reading there is a party wall, however,

118

the wall stands entirely on the parcel of the building next door. In such event, it would be necessary and prudent to obtain affirmative insurance from the title company that it would insure the party wall for so long as the building might stand. Otherwise, if your neighbor took down "his" building, you could lose a wall of yours.

- A survey reading might also disclose that if a house, or garage were built on a boundary line, that the line would perhaps exceed it by some portion of the building. It is not uncommon to see a variance of up to six inches. Again, in such instance, affirmative insurance must be requested from the title company, since the company does not ordinarily give it in the absence of a request.

- It is also possible that the survey reading will show that fire escapes overhang the street (encroachment) or that a neighbor's house or garage or fence or swings, encroach on the parcel being bought, sold, or mortgaged. In each instance, each item raised in the survey reading needs to be checked to ascertain whether it is consistent with the deed. If not, it may be necessary to get or give an easement to or from a neighbor or even deed over or receive a portion of property to clear the property line.

 The affirmative insurance that is referred to in these examples is usually available at no charge, or for a very modest increase in premium. It's worth it, because if you don't ask for the insurance, it isn't ordinarily supplied. If you have the coverage, it gives great peace of mind and helps on eventual resale. A review of a survey will mean different things to different people. Are the boundaries what you thought you were purchasing? Does the survey raise another issue (e.g., does a fence located inside a boundary line raise an issue of adverse possession)? Some of this is intuitive, other aspects of it require some knowledge of real property law.

RESOLVING READING PROBLEMS

If a survey reading is compared with the actual survey (as it must be to properly review a title certificate), any differences must be resolved. For example, if a house is a two-and-a-half-story frame and the survey reading discloses that it is a two-story house, this difference needs to be resolved; a typical resolution is for either the survey reading to be corrected or for the survey to be corrected. What is not permissible is an inconsistence—your review of a survey, and the survey reading itself, should be identical.

SURVEY INSPECTIONS

A survey inspection is done in conjunction with certain types of title insurance that lenders require. It means that as part of the insuring the title, a person is sent out to actually inspect the property. Typically, a survey inspection is not required if a survey is less than six months old. Even there, however, it is often prudent for a survey inspection although there is usually a modest additional cost since it requires an in-person visit to the property and a comparison (usually) between what is shown on the survey, and the actual appearance of the land and improvements. Survey inspections sometimes disclose surprises. For example, if the survey were to show a house and a garage (separate) and a survey were to disclose the same, a survey inspection might disclose that the garage has had three feet added to it even though it otherwise looks the same; an astute practitioner will utilize this, then, to ascertain whether (for the "addition" to the garage) a building permit was obtained and a certificate of occupancy issued (if that is required by local authorities). A survey inspection may also disclose that a two-and-a-half-story house has become a three-story house through the addition of a dormer (again, this is a clue to ask for information on a certificate of occupancy, building permits, and so forth).

 If you don't ask and make the purchase, there may be no problem for years. Then, one of your neighbors will have a fight with you and complain to the building inspector. You'll say it was that way when you purchased it—but that's not a defense to a building violation. You could be required to tear down the improvement and restore it at your own expense, or to go to the time and effort of applying for a variance.

A survey inspection may show the removal of a shed, the demolition of a garage, enclosure of a former screened-in porch, the addition of a fence at or near the property line (sometimes "not located" in the inspection) or myriad other improvements to the parcel. Typically, a survey inspection is undertaken by the title company, or abstract company, and is not intended to show defects in an improvement, but merely to generally describe them; for example, if a screened-in porch had partially collapsed but was otherwise drawn as it appeared on the original survey, this would not show, nor would it be reported; if a driveway, formerly gravel, was paved in the identical spot, this wouldn't be reported, typically, on a survey inspection.

 One way to save money is to ask the lender if it's possible to utilize the old survey, and to have a survey inspection ordered. On residential property, the surveyor simply visits the property and checks to be certain that there are no changes from the original survey. If there are changes, the surveyor reports whether they are within the boundaries of the property. Your savings for this service can be substantial compared with the cost of a new survey.

 A survey inspection can be used together with an affidavit, signed by the current owner, that there have been no changes in the parcel since they acquired it, and that the old survey is correct, as is. (Regardless, you want this read into your title report, if possible. In some instances, especially on commercial properties, it is no longer possible to obtain a survey inspection, and a new survey must be ordered.)

Helpful Hint If you have a new survey done, be sure that the surveyor marks the dimensions and distance from your house to all outer points of the property. There may be no need for it, now, but if you ever expand the house, your local zoning board—or the building inspector—may require the information. By having it on the survey, in advance, you're saving yourself time and money, later. It doesn't cost anything more to have it done, now. What you want to ask the surveyor to do is to show front yard and side yard setbacks and the distance from the rear of the house to the back of the lot line.

For most condominium purchases, particularly in newer buildings, you do not need a separate survey. Typically, a master survey will have been done when the building was built, which will show how the building lays on the land, and an interior survey will show how each unit is laid out. You should ask to have this survey read into any policy for title insurance that you obtain in connection with the purchase.

Be sure to obtain an extra copy or two of the survey and reading, signed and sealed by the surveyor, at the time that you make your purchase. It will save time and money when it comes time to sell the property, and you can negotiate with the buyer for the use of this as a money-saver to them.

Chapter 27

What Is a "Tax Description" and "Tax Search"? Why Are They Important to Me?

Land taxes have been part and parcel of ownership of real property for hundreds of years. The Magna Carta signed at Runnymede was initiated, in part, because of a perception that King John was unfairly taxing his barons on their land. The tax description contained in a Certificate and Report of Title reflects the municipal boundaries utilized for the purposes of taxation on a parcel of land.

A tax search checks the records to see that past taxes have been paid and to determine if future taxes have been assessed and how much they are. (Failure to pay land taxes can result in the forfeiture of your property to the municipality. Therefore, getting an accurate tax description goes hand in hand with being fairly taxed.)

When you purchase real estate, your real estate contract will typically call for taxes to be prorated either at the closing or at some other agreed-on date. Proration means that you will pay that portion of the taxes falling due during your period of ownership while the other party will do same for their period of ownership.

For example, if taxes are collected quarterly in your community and you purchase a residence on August 1, the taxes due July 1 should already have been paid. The July 1 tax payment covers the months of July, August, and September. You would therefore be required to reimburse the seller for the two months that were paid, but unused.

 Many times, lawyers or escrow companies who handle a closing will adjust taxes, water, and sewer and other similar charges by dividing the value shown by 360, and then coming up with a per diem charge. The use of 360 is left over from a precomputer age when calculators were a rarely portable luxury, and almost always were expensive. It was easier to divide by 360 than by the true 365 or 366 days in a given year. (There are 366 days in a leap year.) If this is the case, you can usually save a few dollars by insisting that 365 days a year be used as the point of division. (The amount that you save is .003794 cents per hundred dollars. On a typical adjustment of $3,500 for taxes, the suggestion would just about pay for the cost of this book.)

TAX DESCRIPTIONS

In some instances, the tax description will actually be in a skeletal survey form. It is never a substitute for a survey, because it affords no guarantee as to its accuracy—only that the parcel (as sized) is being taxed. It is not unusual for the tax description to vary slightly from the survey description. For example, if a parcel is 50 feet by 100 feet, rectangular, the tax parcel might be 50 feet by 100.06 feet.

Typically, where the difference between the tax description and the survey and legal description (metes and bounds) is less than 6 inches off, there is not a problem because most statutes recognize that whereas the surveyor's instruments are precise, a builder's trowel isn't. If the tax description differs significantly, however, there can be a major problem: If the tax description of the parcel is too small, portions of the parcel may be part of another tax block and lot, which might have gone "in rem" and be in danger of forfeiture to the state as a consequence of failure to pay land and realty taxes.

In rural areas, tax descriptions are frequently referred to simply by block and lot, which parallels closely the survey; caution should be used to ascertain that the tax block and lot is the same as the land map block and lot. It is not always the case.

- A tax description that describes only a portion of your parcel needs to be corrected. Otherwise, someone else's failure to pay taxes—on your land—could cause you to lose your property at a tax sale.

- If the tax description is accurate, then the tax search for that block and lot can be easily examined to ascertain payment or nonpayment. If it is incorrect or differs significantly, you need to contact the title company to ascertain the reason for the discrepancy. It must be cleared up prior to closing.

- If the tax description is correct, you then need to examine the tax search. If the tax description is partially complete, and partially incomplete (for example, one tax lot is included, and another is not) you can partially continue to examine the title.

However, it will be necessary eventually to have all of the tax lots listed.

MULTIPLE PARCELS

Sometimes, particularly when someone has assembled several plots of land into a single parcel, there still may be multiple tax blocks and lots. Unless the individual goes through a specific tax proceeding to merge the tax block and lots into a single lot, this is almost always the case. This does not pose a problem; however, it does necessitate (with respect to the tax search) assuring that all of the monies due and owing are paid.

 If you have multiple parcels that are adjacent to each other, your lender may charge you a lower tax servicing fee if the parcels are merged. Consider this option if it makes sense.

KEEPING NOTES

It is useful to make note of the tax block and lot that is part of the description in a place that you can access later, long after the closing. It should be endorsed on the inside cover of the file that you set up as follows: "Block so-and-so, Lot such-and-such." The reason is that any dealings that you have with a county or local municipality concerning the land will need to use the block and lot description. The tax block and lot will be utilized on the deed, on the mortgage, on any refinancing that you may do in the future, and in a variety of other instruments. Its convenient source will facilitate future reference.

Helpful Hint It is also helpful to keep with your address book a separate entry listing the parcel of land involved (typically by street address, as well as other identifying features); it is especially useful to have the tax block and lot contained since often (years after the fact) information about the parcel can be retrieved simply by knowing the block and lot. If you don't keep these records, you'll probably have to go to the county clerk that indexes property, spending time and money to find information that's at your fingertips when you start.

Chapter 28

Why Should I Worry about Covenants, Conditions, and Restrictions?

Prior to the time of King Henry VIII of England, the concept of a restriction on the land's use was unknown in Anglo-Saxon law. In the 32nd year of Henry's reign in 1540, a law was passed allowing covenants to freely affect land provided there was consent from the acquiring party. Its purpose was to deal with the lands of the Catholic monasteries that were being disenfranchised and distributed.

Today, covenants, conditions, and restrictions are typically written into the deeds of almost every parcel of land, not to restrict monasteries, but instead to regulate development, zoning, or other attributes associated with the contour of the land.

In a housing subdivision, covenants may deal with anything from the type of roofing material that may be used, to the minimum square footage allowed when building. They can restrict your ability to erect a fence, or even place a hot tub or swimming pool in your yard. They can restrict the colors that your house can be painted on the outside, and prohibit you from maintaining a commercial office or business in your home, however innocuous. Although covenants and restrictions are usually done by deed, they can be stricken, or granted, judicially.

It's important to understand that covenants, conditions, and restrictions usually (but not always) run with the land. This means that when you sell a property, you can't remove them for the new buyer. It also means the buyer must abide by them. To change or remove covenants, conditions, and restrictions, short of going to court, requires the consent of all parties to the change (everyone in the subdivision) and, often, that of a local planning board or commission as well.

Sometimes, a contemporary covenant is written to obtain a zoning variance. For example, a board of zoning or adjustment may require, as a condition for granting a zoning variance, that a covenant, condition, or restriction be granted to provide some important relief that the town thinks essential. For example, this might involve limiting a particular use (such as a two-family house) to an owner's lifetime.

TYPES OF COVENANTS, CONDITIONS, AND RESTRICTIONS

There are a number of different types of covenants, conditions, and restrictions. They are used, for example, to improve the quality of a neighborhood. This (typically) is a covenant that precludes an animal-rendering plant; a slaughterhouse; a gunpowder factory; a site where ink is made, and so forth. The terminology is usually quite simple, and repetitive.

Covenants, conditions, and restrictions may also be used to require something to be done or to prohibit something. Here are several examples:

- Plantings in the front yard.
- Placing fences anywhere on the parcel.
- Operating businesses in a residential area.
- Premises from falling into disrepair.
- Access to premises (through easements, for example).
- Failure to make repairs.
- Agreements relative to improvements.

Many years ago, there were also covenants that ran with the land for the express purpose of preventing a certain type of people from settling a particular area. These were frequently in the form of a covenant that prohibited selling real estate to people of a certain ethnic or racial group. The Supreme Court declared in *Shelley v. Kraemer* 334 U.S. 1 (1948) that these were unconstitutional, and they are no longer in effect, even if they still run with the land.

In certain parts of the country, it is not uncommon for a title company to disclose a recorded restriction that prohibits sale of land to Jews, or to Negroes (in the vernacular of the time in which each was written); they are void and unenforceable. Most often, the Certificate and Report of Title will attach a copy of the covenant and restriction and state where it is reported. Where the covenant and restriction is especially old, sometimes it is not easily reproducible. In such event, the Certificate and Report of Title typically will recite the covenant.

THE EFFECT OF COVENANTS, CONDITIONS, AND RESTRICTIONS

The covenant is an encumbrance upon the land—it diminishes its value, even though it is intended to enhance it. The diminution is that it is a limitation on the free alienation (sale) of the property. From the standpoint of a purchaser, or from a borrower or even a lender, there is also a danger of a "reversionary interest." If the use of the premises—at the time of the sale or the mortgage—were somehow found to violate the covenant, the land would conceivably revert to the grantor.

It is thus customary to request affirmative insurance from the title company. You want the affirmative insurance to be certain that you are purchasing property that isn't going to revert—and cause you to lose your investment.

 Affirmative insurance might read [a certain use is prohibited] except that the company insures that the current use does not violate such restrictive covenant, and that any subsequent use will not result in reversion. Covenants, conditions, and restrictions declared illegal (such as those precluding individuals of a particular race, or religion, from acquiring the property) are nonetheless, because they were reported, part of the history of the land, and almost always require affirmative insurance.

COVENANTS, CONDITIONS, AND RESTRICTIONS AND EASEMENTS

Sometimes a covenant, condition, or restriction will also involve an easement. For example, a descriptive easement or an easement by necessity may have at some time or another been agreed on between two parties, and reported. Where a parcel requires access to a street, frequently, a title company can be asked for—and will grant—affirmative insurance approximately as follows: "Access to the nearest street is insured."

PERSONAL COVENANT

A covenant may run with the land or be personal, binding only the person issuing the covenant and those with knowledge of the restrictions.

The key is the intention of the parties, and the manner in which the covenant is written in the first place, since a binding covenant must be recorded.

COVENANTS, CONDITIONS, AND RESTRICTIONS TO WATCH FOR

In each deed, there are typically five separate covenants, conditions, and restrictions that may not be violated without substantial damages being incurred by the owner of the property:

Helpful Hint The right to convey premises (sometimes called the Covenant of Seisin).

Helpful Hint The right to quiet enjoyment of the premises.

Helpful Hint Freedom from encumbrances when transferred.

Helpful Hint Further assurances (meaning that the grantor of the deed will execute or procure any reasonable or necessary further assurance of the title). This is in the nature of a future obligation to prospective purchasers.

Helpful Hint Warranty of title (under which the seller forever warrants that he or she had good title to the premises). It is useful to remember that a covenant can have a positive effect on your property.

Suppose that you are dividing your property in half and want to sell off a portion. But you want to be sure that all that is ever built on the portion sold is a one-family residence. A covenant, condition, and restriction can accomplish this goal for you.

 If you have a portion of your property that a neighbor needs such as access to a proposed new driveway over a part of your lot, you can sell the use to your neighbor (but not the property, itself) and record a covenant allowing it to be used for perpetuity, or for a shorter period. Usually, this is a moneymaker for the person granting the rights.

Chapter 29

Why Is a Street Report Important?

A street report is strictly informational describing any of the streets that abut or are in close proximity to a property. One of the elements of importance is to ascertain whether the street is legally opened. If a street is not legally opened, it may well be that the value of the land is substantially diminished; but typically, even a landlocked parcel has easement rights that allow you to get in and out (ingress and egress).

All streets in a large city like New York, in the borough of Manhattan, are legally open and are dedicated to their full width. This is not true, however, in some of the outer boroughs of New York and, in rural areas, may not be true at all. The purpose of a street report, therefore, is to assure you of being able to properly secure and utilize a parcel; to be able to gain access to and from the parcel to the nearest legally open street.

STREET REPORT PROBLEMS

A street report may come back and indicate that the parcel is on a street, 60 feet wide, that is not legally dedicated. This means that the street in essence is "private," and may be owned by an individual or other group, or, it may be owned by the homeowner. In this situation, the city may have the right to take the street by means of condemnation. A lender in almost every instance will want insurance, first, that the streets are legally opened; second, that if the streets are not legally opened, the lender will be fully insured by the title company in the event of a taking by condemnation; and third, that in the event of such a taking, the parcel will not be diminished in value.

WHAT TO DO

- If you find a bargain that eventually proves to be a problem because of an ingress or egress issue as determined by a street report, or even if it's just a street that is not fully widened, you may not be able to get title insurance to cover that issue.

Don't be afraid to ask for it, however. Don't simply pass on property because of the problem. This may occur when an "interior" parcel is purchased. In almost every instance, a title company will insure access to the nearest street, or to some legally open street, if the prospective insured makes that request.

- In some instances, although a street may be "mapped" according to the final map of a particular town or borough at 60 feet wide, it is only legally open to 40 feet; this means that the city has condemned the first 40 feet of the parcel consisting of the street but has not acquired the remaining 20 feet (typically, 10 feet on each side). Where the city or municipality has failed to acquire title to all of the street, or actually the street bed, it does not necessarily mean that they will want to do so. To acquire title to a street, a condemnation proceeding is required, and this can cost a significant amount of money. You may be just fine with things the way they are! For example, throughout the 1970s and the 1980s, the City of New York was not undertaking condemnation actions for streets. This does not mean, of course, they may not do so in the future; hence, the need for affirmative insurance.
- You should be aware that it may not be as necessary for you to be protected as for a lender.

 Lenders, particularly banks, often use all kinds of creative insurance, based on the perceived risk of the title company. Like most other kinds of affirmative insurance, it is available at no increase in the regular rate. On the other hand, if you're the lender (for example, a seller taking back paper), insist on coverage that allows access from the nearest legally opened street; if you're an owner (or buyer), ask for the coverage. It will save you time and money when it comes time to eventually resell.

WHAT TO CHECK FOR

- In looking at the street report, it is important to compare the names of the streets listed in the street report as being adjacent, or abutting, and to check these as against the survey. On occasion, an improper street report is given (i.e., a street report with the names of abutting streets is not correct). In such event, a new street report is required, and the title company needs to be so apprised.

- You should always check the street report yourself against the listing of byways that can be found on the survey, itself. Each street that either abuts the parcel, or is in close proximity as a cross-street, should be listed on the street report, together with a statement as to whether or not the street is legally opened, and to its full width. If it isn't, you can still get Fannie Mae approved loans, provided that the title company is willing to give affirmative insurance that the owner of the parcel, and the mortgagor, will have access to the nearest paved road, or street.

Chapter 30

What Is an Easement and How Can It Affect Me?

An easement is the right of one property owner to use the land or property of another property owner for his or her own purposes. It may be of a reciprocal nature, or an easement of necessity. A negative easement may prohibit certain actions on the lands or property of another. Easements exist for purposes of access to land. They include:

- The right of way over one parcel of land (owned by a different landowner) to the land of another.
- A parcel's ability to obtain light, which might otherwise be blocked.
- Ability of land to have access to air, which may sound ridiculous in some contexts, but is important in a city where the habitability of a parcel (or apartment) could be called into question if the surrounding air was cut off.
- Water rights upstream, downstream, and even that of people to cross land to be able to swim in a lake.
- Support for adjacent land or property, where soil may not be removed if it will remove the ground support for an adjacent parcel.
- Utilities, who want to cross your land (above or underground) with pipes or cables. Easements typically do not to diminish the rights—or the interests—of a mortgagee. They do diminish the rights of the owner of a parcel.

CREATING AN EASEMENT

Easements are usually created by written declaration that is recorded in the county or state land office, usually by a county clerk, and designate a burden on one piece of land for the benefit of another piece of land. They can also be created by habit or practice, or even by necessity that is uncontested.

A neighbor who wants an easement typically pays for the right to use your land with a one-time charge. If you intend for this to go on forever, an easement is the typical solution.

- Licenses may be created as well, but a license is a form of contract that is not typically implied by the law, whereas an easement can be granted by a court even if the party whose parcel is to be burdened with the easement doesn't consent. An annual or monthly renewal of the right is usually done if a license is granted.

- Sometimes, particularly in the western United States, an easement is created to obtain mineral rights. Other times, a prior owner simply reserves the right to mine minerals from the land at the time that it is sold. The strangest easement that either of us have ever seen was officially reported as being an easement to use the chimney of another house. The easement also allowed a commercial property owner to use the toilet facilities of his neighbor, necessary because of the way that a property that was once a single entity was split in two.

WATCH OUT FOR EASEMENTS

All easements must be carefully reviewed by a prospective purchaser, read by the title company and lender, and analyzed. Sometimes an opinion may be sought from the title company as to what liability, if any, may result. Your title company has an obligation to inform you at the time of purchase of all easements that have been recorded, and hence are "of record."

 If you later discover an easement that you were not made aware of at the time of the closing, the value of your land will be diminished, and the title company may pay you for the diminution in value. Frequently, as a purchaser you may also want to secure an opinion from an attorney as to what rights the easement gives you, and what rights it may take away. When an easement issue turns up in a property that you intend to purchase, or to sell, it is prudent to involve either an attorney or a title company that offers legal advice as to what you need to obtain title insurance.

- Get the opinion in writing! You may not need it until years later. Many purchasers of land (first-time home buyers, in particular) have little understanding about easements and their importance. If you fall into this group, be wary. Find out whether there are any easements and what their consequences may be. Also, make every effort to obtain affirmative title insurance covering the easement. That makes the parcel more valuable to the lender, and ultimately to the owner.

 You can also turn your property into a moneymaker if someone wants to use it to get better access to their property. Instead of selling them the adjacent land, you simply license them to go over it; if you regularize this so that it can always be done—and this is usually paid for handsomely—you've created an easement.

Chapter 31

What Do I Do When I'm Selling a House and the Title Search Turns Up Judgments against Me?

A significant part of any title report is a listing of judgments found against the seller (or even the purchaser) of the parcel. If judgments are found, in all probability they will need to be removed prior to closing the sale because a lender won't fund a new mortgage until they are no longer of record.

Even if the lender would fund, it's highly desirable that they be removed for the peace of mind of the buyer. The reason for this is that in the event a sale takes place without the removal, the purchasers won't get clear title. (They won't be able to convey at a later date without removal of this impediment.)

Technically, they are not bona fide purchasers for "value, without notice." The judgment serves as the notice, provided it is properly docketed and recorded. (This means docketed in a superior court,* and in some instances, certain inferior state courts.) In effect, the buyers would take title subject to the judgment—and the judgment creditor might have rights to sell off the parcel to satisfy the judgment. Several different types of judgments typically turn up.

Helpful Hint The most common judgment is against someone with a similar name, who lives at a different address (or even the same address) but is not the seller of the parcel, the mortgagor, or the purchaser. People with similar names are far more common than might be imagined, and even names in other languages that appear obscure to us are sometimes more common than might be imagined; judgments are frequently found against these people. Where the person cited in the certificate report title is there simply because his or her name is the same as the name of one of the

---

*States use a variety of names to encompass this type of court. In New York, it is the Supreme Court; in New Jersey, the Superior Court.

parties involved in the transaction, most title companies will accept an affidavit from the affected party to that transaction. The affidavit states in substance as follows:

> My name is similar to that which appears in a certain certificate and report of title issued by the title company on [date]. Therein, the following judgments are listed against the individual named, in the amount stated, and at the court indicated. I am not this individual, inasmuch as I have never resided at the address listed nor am I indebted to the judgment creditor in that action. This affidavit is made for the purpose of inducing the title insurer to omit from the policy of title insurance such judgments, and I am aware that should such claim be improperly omitted, that I am subject to punishment and financial penalty.

Helpful Hint In the five boroughs in the City of New York, the most common judgment is from the Parking Violations Bureau. Where the seller actually has a judgment entered against him or her, a satisfaction must be issued; in the case of a judgment from the Parking Violations Bureau, a certificate of disposition is required.

 If you have ever gotten a parking ticket, or do get one, be certain that you retain proof of payment or disposition. This will save you a lot of time and money in terms of showing that the obligation is in fact satisfied. You may still be required to obtain a certificate of satisfaction or disposition. You should retain these in a common file so that you can access them, when necessary.

A certificate of disposition can only be issued by the Parking Violations Bureau, and the title company will inevitably require its production at the closing (as opposed to filing it in a different manner with an applicable court).

There may be other types of judgments against the sellers. Perhaps they were cosigners on an auto loan years ago and the primary borrower defaulted and the car was repossessed. The lender may have secured a deficiency judgment against the sellers and recorded it on their property. Regardless of the cause of the judgment, it must be removed. The procedure can be simple or time consuming, can be handled by an individual or, in complex cases where a court appearance may be necessary, may require the assistance of an attorney.

Our suggestion is that you first try to resolve the issue by contacting the person who placed the judgment on the property. If it was a mistake, they may be willing to correct it. If money is owed, they very likely will agree to a release, provided they are paid, often at close from monies out of escrow. In most cases, only if no resolution seems possible through a commonsense approach, will you need to proceed with an attorney.

Ownership of Real Property

Chapter 32

Can I Avoid Probate by Owning Real Property as a Joint Tenancy?

Probably, at least for a time. Probate is the legal transfer of property from a decedent to the heirs and legatees, after provision has been made to pay the legitimate creditors of the estate. While probate refers both to real and personal property, if you own real estate, it's often going to eventually require probating so that the tax man receives his due. More than 450 years ago, Shakespeare put it bluntly in *King Richard II* "Let's choose executors and talk of wills." A will is the instrument of probate; absent one, administration takes place (to also transfer property).

TITLE TO PROPERTY

Property can be owned in one of three ways, if more than one person is involved, all relating to how transfer is handled upon death. As a tenant in common (or as a tenant in partnership), in which case the property remains the property of its individual owners or their estates after they die. As tenants by the entirety or community property (available to married couples, only, in which the principal residence of the couple passes automatically to the other upon death). And as a joint tenancy with right of survivorship, in which a right of survivorship passes the property on to the surviving owner.

PASSING TITLE UPON DEATH

Where property is held in joint tenancy, or as a tenancy by the entirety, it passes automatically to the other party upon death. If the other party is a spouse, the property is given a "stepped up" basis and no immediate tax is due. If the other party is not a spouse, the estate of the decedent has obligations to pay taxes that may be due on it, hence probate. Probate is generally not required when the only asset of an estate is the marital residence, and that is owned as a tenancy by the entirety, thus passing to the spouse on the death of the other. If the spouse continues to hold the property, or even if he or she wishes to sell it, the joint tenancy will at that time obviate the necessity of having a formal probate proceeding—provided that the rest of the assets in the estate are moderate and don't otherwise reach the state's minimal standard for assessing taxes, or exceed the federal government's $600,000 exemption.

When the successor spouse dies, however, and is still the owner of the property, the property then must be probated before the heirs (or legatees) can receive their shares. This is merely the law. A host of other entities and groups may have a different view, depending on what is subsequently done with the property. These include:

- The title company that is being asked to insure title in a subsequent transaction, typically involving Individual, as surviving joint tenant, transfer to X, a new purchaser. The title company may ask for probate proceedings or a tax waiver. You'll have to supply it to give insurable title.

- A lending institution, if the surviving tenant seeks to place a mortgage on the premises, or to refinance an existing one. They may also require a formal probate to give judicial imprimatur to the ownership change.

- An estate's lawyer or the surviving partner or spouse's lawyer, which may have to do with certain ongoing liabilities or obligations associated with the parcel.

- Governmental authorities, who may require transfer if applications are made for certain purposes, as for example an amendment to the certificate of occupancy.

DEFERRING PROBATE

Deferring probate, typically, omits the tax that might otherwise have to be paid immediately. (There is no tax, on a federal level, of joint tenancy property that passes from one spouse to another.) But there will be an ultimate day of reckoning, since eventually, the death of the second spouse will cause probate to take place.

Helpful Hint   A familiar law school riddle is to ask whether a surviving tenant, by remarrying, could forever avoid probate (and taxation). The answer is theoretically yes, but in practice, when the chain breaks as it surely will, a tax becomes due.

 If the property is sold by the second spouse, cashing out the position, it is possible that probate may be avoided altogether. However, a title company may still require probate of assets to give clean title in a deed of sale.

 If a spouse is the recipient and remarries, and deeds the property into the joint name of both spouses, it is theoretically possible to delay the probate for a substantial period.

 If your gross estate exceeds $600,000—presently the largest amount that you can legally have without having to file a federal return—you must disclose on Form 706 (the federal estate tax return) joint tenancy property. Also, prudent estate planning often uses a variety of sophisticated tax-saving devices that involve payment of taxes now, rather than later. Once the tax is paid by one spouse, for example, it is possible to down-shift the income to the next generation tax free.

 If you do take title as joint tenants, be certain that you keep good records. Be certain that you have the deed, a copy of the mortgage and mortgage note, and your closing statement—together with a listing of improvements that you make in the premises over the years that follow. This will help lower your taxes when you sell the premises or are challenged at the audit level by a revenue authority.

Chapter 33

How Can I End the Co-Ownership of Real Estate When the Other Co-Owner Doesn't Want To?

If you are the owner of real estate with another person, whether as a tenant in common, a joint tenant with right of survivorship, or a tenant in partnership, the day may well come when you want to dispose of the real estate and find, much to your dismay, that your co-owner is in serious disagreement with you.

For more than 450 years—since the time of King Henry VIII of England—the law has provided a remedy for this: partition. It involves physically dividing the real estate, if possible, or if not possible, selling the property and sharing the proceeds with the warring factions.

Partition is an ancient, equitable remedy that has been modernized by statute and is available either statutorily or voluntarily. It is used when the parties own property jointly, or when one party or another has a legal interest that may be separated from the whole. It may be done by deed, by agreement (sometimes oral or written), or by action. It can involve large parcels of land, where it seems fairly obvious that division can be accomplished, or a commercial office that is owned, for example, by two physicians—where a wall has to be built or a common reception area retained.

It's important to remember, however, that the concept behind partition begins with the almost unique Anglo-Saxon idea of property ownership, and the desire not take property away from any owner lightly.

GUIDELINES TO CONSIDER IN ANY PARTITION ACTION

- When it is possible to divide the property but not to maintain the value in an even fashion, the difference is called "owelty," and the co-owner who gets the better "half" has to compensate the other for the privilege.

- Because partition takes away property ownership, this procedure is inevitably time consuming, expensive, and fraught with paperwork.
- When two or more partners own real estate together, and run it as a partnership venture, they cannot achieve partition by an involuntary sale of the parcel. The proper remedy is for them to seek dissolution of the partnership.
- A husband or wife cannot seek partition of property that is owned by them as tenants by the entirety. However, once divorced, the parties can seek involuntary judicial partition of premises that they previously owned, unless prohibited expressly in their separation agreement or divorce decree.

 If you are contemplating a separation or divorce from your spouse, and own real property together, it is better (faster and less expensive) to provide for a transfer of title as part of the matrimonial proceeding than to do so by partition.

DETERMINING THE PROPERTY'S VALUE

To establish the value of a parcel, in whole or in part, statutes frequently require that three disinterested commissioners or referees be appointed by the court to determine value. Since they must be landowners themselves, it is presumed that they will understand the difficulty in dividing or valuing property.

PARTICIPANTS IN PARTITION ACTIONS

Partition is available for the following persons or situations:

- Tenants in common.
- Owners as joint tenants with right of survivorship.
- Conservatorship.
- Life tenants (as to their interest); a tenant for years as to his or her interest generally cannot have that interest partitioned.
- Corporations that own property with others. A tenancy by partnership cannot be partitioned; the proper remedy is to dissolve the partnership.

- Property owned by trusts.
- Improvements to real property.
- Mining claims.

SHOULD YOU SEEK AN ATTORNEY OR DO IT YOURSELF?

Partition actions are not for the fainthearted. They can be costly and difficult, and may require expert (read attorney) help (particularly if the other party resists). They are also very time consuming. It is not unheard of for them to drag on for years, and, if the result is inequitable, for an appellate court to become the successor battlesite. Sometimes, however, if the other owner is obstinate, the simple threat of partition—and even the initiation of litigation concerning it—can result in a settlement. (It may take the litigation to convince the other party of your determination and of the costs and consequences of resisting.)

Even if not initially achieved, the use of this litigation vehicle can cause the other side to resolve the matter (or to settle it) rather than take the chance on what commissioners might do, or what a court might award for equalization. Partition is not a panacea, but rather an avenue of last resort that may be utilized to get your money out of a parcel—or to give you your share of it—when there are no better alternatives. Remember, it is time consuming and costly, and many times can be utilized as a tactic in litigation, a means to achieve an end, rather than the desired end, itself.

Chapter 34

How Can I Purchase a House with My Companion?

With the same care that you would undertake if you were about to enter into a business partnership with a stranger.

When husband and wife purchase a residence, they typically take title as tenants by the entirety or as community property, a method of property ownership that exists only in the context of marriage. Alternative lifestyle arrangements presently do not have the same protection afforded as a tenancy by the entirety does.

Further, if a marriage dissolves, the partners in that economic unit have the basic protection that the law provides—equitable distribution of assets. That safeguard also is unavailable to companions, whether they be mere business partners, lovers, couples, or special companions.

Given these circumstances, smart joint purchasers enter into such a large economic transaction the same way that they would act if they were purchasing a large office building or a corporate jet plane: They have an agreement that defines the relationship including the rights, obligations, and liabilities of each participant.

They also focus on how the relationship may be terminated and what the economic consequences or liabilities of the parties will then be. It really doesn't matter how long you have been involved in a nonmarital relationship; you need a written agreement to define your rights and liabilities. (There is a growing body of professionals who believe that even in a marriage, the rights should be defined instead of being left to chance.) Here are some of the things you should consider in reaching an understanding with a partner to purchase real estate in which you both intend to reside (or that you intend to utilize as an investment property).

- How will the property be titled: as joint tenants with right of survivorship (if one dies, the other inherits the balance of the parcel, without need of a will); as tenants in common (each with an undivided share of the whole); as tenants in partnership, or corporately (with each individual owning a portion of the shares in the company)?

- What share will each participant have in the property? Will it be equal?
- What share will each contribute to the down payment and to closing expenses?
- What share will each contribute to postclosing expenses (e.g., mortgage payment each month, heat, taxes, electricity, maintenance expenses).
- If one partner doesn't contribute, and the other pays, what are the rights of each partner? For how long may those rights be exercised? Are they recoverable only when the premises are sold, or can they be recovered sooner?
- Who is responsible for day-to-day management of the property?
- If the partners deadlock on either a payment or a decision affecting the property, how should this be resolved?
- Who is entitled to take what share of the tax deduction that the property creates?
- If one of the parties simply walks away, what rights (or special rights) does the other party have?
- Will the credit of one or both be used to obtain the mortgage?

Because purchasing a house is such a large economic transaction, it is important to consider all of the consequences, even years later, that might not be readily apparent at the time that the transaction is entered into. This is important if one of the parties, at a much later point in time, changes the nature of the relationship, or withdraws from it entirely. Whether couples in alternative lifestyles are involved, or any other arrangement in which one or more of the partners will be residing in the residence, it is necessary to decide what the living and sleeping arrangements will be, and to commit them to paper. There are a number of other caveats that partners of every gender should carefully consider before undertaking the transaction of a lifetime.

OTHER CONSIDERATIONS

- When the partners are a couple, and the house can accommodate a couple only, think about what you might want to do if you are no longer one couple, but break up and have an extended relationship with other people—in effect, two couples. Is the house susceptible to partition? If it is (see Chapter 33), you may want to expressly prevent this type of a split-up, and provide for a cash buyout.

- If you have a multiple-family house, and you and your partner share an apartment, who will be responsible for maintaining the other apartment for the proverbial leaky faucet in the middle of the night, and who will pay for the rental income from that apartment between tenancies?

- If you have significant differences with your partner, how will you resolve the dispute? Dishrags or spitballs at 10 paces? Litigation? Or do you prefer arbitration (see the first volume in this series—*The 90 Second Lawyer,* by R. Irwin and D. L. Ganz, New York: Wiley, 1996, for extensive information about arbitration).

- Who is going to be responsible for paying the bills? Does it make sense to set up a joint house account to cover the various regular payments and contingencies?

- If the entity that you are purchasing depends on other tenants (i.e., a multifamily house or apartment complex), do you have the economic wherewithal to withstand tenants who are slow-pays, or worse, no-pays?

- If you're going to have tenants, one of you should be designated as the point person. That way, there is no misunderstanding—and the tenant won't be able to do what you and your siblings used to try and do with your parents: play one off against the other.

 Divide any tax considerations wisely (property taxes and mortgage interest on a home). The deductions are worth more to the partner who makes more. If you earn $12,000 a year and your partner earns $70,000, it stands to reason your partner will be taxed at the highest marginal rate, rather than at your lowest. Giving partner the tax advantages maximizes the savings.

 Is the premises being purchased your joint residence, a vacation home, or something that is merely an investment property? Decisions that will affect the property subsequently will flow from what is being purchased. Think in advance about what might be an issue between you and your companion if you are no longer friendly, or not together, but find yourselves as investment partners in unwanted property. What would you want to do? What would you want to have happen? Think about this, and write it into your agreement, now.

 The real money-saver in acquiring a property with a companion is in drawing up an agreement between yourselves as to the obligations, rights, duties, and responsibilities of the parties, and taking care, in advance, to state how the union will be dissolved. You can do this without a lawyer by simple letter agreement or you can have something more formal prepared.

Chapter 35

Valuables Were Stolen from My Home: What Do I Do?

Ouch! The good news is that you may have an insurance and/or tax claim to file. Suppose you've been a rare stamp collector for several years and have put together a nice collection. Although you usually keep your stamps in the bank vault, some pieces in the collection are in your den at home one day when suddenly you discover that several have been lost or stolen (or perhaps taken in a burglary).

Of course, instead of a rarity it could be jewelry or even a TV set. What do you do?

First, call your insurance company and immediately set up a chronological file on any legal matter. This cannot be overstated.

This means opening a file and placing, chronologically, a copy of each document that thereafter comes into your hands. Not only should you do this, but you should also maintain a list of the people with whom you speak about the claim, including the date (and time), and telephone number that was called, and a brief memo of the conversation. It's also handy to keep copies of documents in reverse chronological order (oldest at the bottom, latest on the top).

If the missing items are insured by you, the insurance broker (and the insurance company) should be placed on written notice about the claim. You can call your broker to initiate action, but always follow up with a written letter, sent by certified mail, return receipt requested. A carbon copy of the same letter, sent to the insurance company, is all that you need to initially protect your rights with them.

WHAT SHOULD THE INITIAL LETTER STATE?

- Your name, address, telephone number (work and home).
- The insurance company that issued the policy.
- The broker's name and address.
- Your policy number (usually listed on the policy itself).

- A brief statement of what occurred.
- Approximate date of occurrence (if known).
- A general statement of what is missing.
- An estimate of the value of the loss with a general statement as to how it is calculated.

 Before you report the loss to your insurance company, look at your policy of insurance. Sometimes, how you characterize a claim will be the basis on which the insurance company pays or declines coverage. Be honest about what occurred but avoid characterizing something as "intentional," which is interpretive, rather than "accidental," which is less subjective. The difference can be coverage versus no coverage.

WITHOUT INSURANCE

On recent claims, you may still be entitled to a theft loss on your tax return. (Even if you have insurance but fail to make the claim, a 1981 Tax Court case involving the Hills family permits a theft loss under Section 165 of the Internal Revenue Code.) Of course, if you recover the cost of your loss through insurance, you can't also file a theft loss on your tax return. In the typical loss, there are two basic problems. The first has to do with the way in which the lost or stolen items are valued. The second relates to proof of loss, and perhaps proof of acquisition in the first place.

Helpful Hint   Records are essential in this aspect of the proceeding including your acquisition records for each of the missing items. If you keep your only inventory list with the items lost or stolen, don't expect a lot of sympathy from the insurance company, or even the Internal Revenue Service.

Helpful Hint   In the case of valuables such as rare coins or jewelry, you may be required to submit a formal appraisal.

Helpful Hint   Even if a formal appraisal is required, you can supply a list of the lost items, their initial cost, and a current price if you can find one, representing the estimated replacement cost.

Helpful Hint   For truly rare or valuable items, a photo of the item as well as a receipt for its cost (or an explanation) is almost always warranted. If you don't have insurance, you'll need to follow the same rules to take the theft loss deduction. In responding to a loss, the key is to be controlled, and not to panic. Don't hesitate to call your accountant or tax professional to discuss the problems and ramifications. Maybe it will never happen, but if it does happen to you, be prepared.

Taking Possession of a Home or Other Real Estate

Chapter 36

Do I Need a Final "Walk-Through"?

It is amazing that the most expensive purchase in your life—the home that you are going to live in for the next seven years, if you're a typical buyer—is usually based on 20 or 30 minutes of surface scrutiny, but that a dress for a cocktail party, or a new business suit you'll wear for the next year or two only, could be the subject of hours of agony, trying different styles, sizes, and prices, before you actually make a purchase.

Certainly more attention is needed by most people before deciding to buy. That includes a thorough inspection of the premises, usually with a home inspector. (The sale should be contingent on your approving the inspection.) In addition, after you've agreed to purchase and the sale has been tailored to your needs, you need a final walk-through to make sure that the property has remained in good repair during the purchase process and that all the changes you have requested have been made and that no new defects have been found.

The walk-through constitutes your last opportunity, prior to the sale, to go through the house that you are going to buy, and to make sure that no major problems have occurred since you fell in love with it.

THE PROCEDURE

Most contracts of sale give a purchaser the right to "walk through" the premises 72 hours prior to closing, and to note any changed conditions or defect, or items that the contract calls for that have not been accomplished. It is important to take this seriously, and to have a checklist so that you omit nothing. You have probably already ordered and participated in an inspection, perhaps by an engineer, which called attention to a number of defects in the house. It's only natural for a large structure with thousands of components to have minor defects, and sometimes major ones.

But chances are you won't remember most of them later on when, presumably, they have been corrected. Write these defects down on a piece of paper and let this become your primary checklist during your final walk-through. If the contract of sale calls for the defect to be fixed or cured, make note of that and check to see that the necessary work has been done. Sign them off one by one. If something hasn't been fixed, you may have to do the work yourself after the purchase is consummated. Not good. On the other hand, discovering a problem still exists only a day or so before escrow closes is also a problem—there may not be time to fix it.

 One alternative is to request a closing adjustment in your favor. If the defect is serious, on the other hand, you can demand the seller resolve the issue before closing the deal.

WHAT'S TO BE EXPECTED

Ordinary wear and tear is to be expected. This means that the oven broiler may require cleaning from last night's soup or roast that spilled, but it does not mean that the broiler can be nonfunctional because of the accident. Here are some items that you should check on a final preclosing walk-through, to satisfy that everything remains in good repair:

- The roof should be free of leaks. If there is an attic, see whether any fresh water stains are visible. New stains could indicate a problem.
- Plumbing and heating should be in good repair. Turn the boiler or furnace on, or turn the heat up, even if it is summertime. You want to know whether the furnace is responsive and in good working order.
- For the plumbing, flush each of the toilets, and turn on each sink.
- Look under the sink to check for leaks, and make certain that the toilet stops running after the bowl is full.
- Turn on each air conditioning unit, or portable heating unit that may be in the house. If the temperature outside is below 50 degrees, the air conditioning probably won't work—though it will blow cold air.

- Check the electric garage door opener and the alarm system to make sure that they respond to the code, and the electronic signal.
- Check the windows to make sure that they open, and that they are not cracked or otherwise in need of repairs.

There will always be some things that are unique to the house that you are buying. Be certain that your inspection/engineering report is your guideline to these elements.

IN NEW CONSTRUCTION

If new construction is involved, be certain that you develop a "punch list" of items. One helpful way to do this is to go room by room, making separately numbered notations. Then, at the time of the closing, make sure that each of these items has been addressed to your satisfaction.

 If some items remain undone, ask that funds be held back from escrow to assure that there will be full and satisfactory performance.

Since the seller must agree for money to be held up, he will be immediately put on notice that something has to be done. It's sure to get him to move quickly to make the repairs. Take the walk slowly and carefully. Take good notes. It could well be one of the most important—and certainly one of the most expensive (if you overlook a problem)—walks you ever take in your life.

USING THE WALK-THROUGH
TO GET OUT OF THE DEAL

It's important to understand that the purpose of the walk-through is to make sure that the property at closing is in the same condition as it was when you first saw it and that all noted problems have been fixed. It is not intended as a way for the buyer to back out of the deal or to reopen negotiations. Nevertheless, some very savvy buyers do just that. They make claims (real or imagined) that the property is not as it was or that a defect hasn't been cured.

Since a lot depends on subjective judgment here, it can be difficult to dispute the claim. Generally speaking, if it is a big dispute, the buyer may refuse to buy and the seller may refuse to let the buyer out of the deal. Against the advice of an agent, the whole mess could end up in litigation. Far more often, a settlement of one sort or another is made. The seller may agree to concessions (either lowering the price, adjusting the terms, or doing additional fix-up work). Or the seller may simply decide that it's not worth the hassle and let the buyer out of the deal. Or, it could get very nasty and end up in court.

If you're a buyer who is planning on using a walk-through as a final leverage point to either get out of the deal or reopen the negotiations, be aware that it's a dangerous ploy that could backfire.

If you're a seller and this happens to you, remember that sticking to your guns and insisting the buyer go through with the deal exactly as previously agreed also has perils.

Sometimes mutual compromise, particularly if the buyer appears to have a legitimate complaint, is the best way out.

Chapter 37

What Is a Certificate of Occupancy and What Effect Does That Have on My Property?

It allows you to move into your house and get your utilities connected. Generally you need one when a house is brand-new, or after it has been condemned (as after a fire or other calamity).

The certificate of occupancy is actually a copy of a document issued by a municipality that authorizes the use of a building for a particular purpose, or more than one purpose. Sometimes, in cases where no certificate permitting occupancy is required, building departments then issue a certificate of completion (indicating construction work has been satisfactorily finished).

WHAT MUST A "CERTIFICATE OF OCCUPANCY" CONTAIN?

Typically, a Certificate of Occupancy (C.O.), in addition to the name of the municipality and the date of its issuance (or amendments), will state the following information:

- A street address for the premises.
- Sometimes, the tax block and lot.
- A modified description, which should be compared with the survey and/or survey reading.
- The use of each portion of the premises, specified by floor. Because a certificate of occupancy is largely informational, rather than a binding legal document, it may differ from area to area, even within the same city. It may even contain some discrepancies and not be considered invalid. For example, the certificate of occupancy may state that constructed on the premises is a two-story frame house. Actual inspection may reveal that there are two main levels to the house, but that there is also a

finished attic. This is considered acceptable for two reasons: First, the certificate of occupancy is merely informational. Second, the half-story attic simply is usually omitted as a matter of building practice.

If the certificate of occupancy does not match either the survey reading, the survey (see Chapter 26), or any other description of the property, it does not adversely affect the title to the property. The second reason is that the certificate may reflect the view of what the improvement on the parcel is in accordance with the building code; a two-and-a-half-story house under most building codes is a standard two-story house with an attic. (A surveyor may interpret an attic with a window as a half-story. The building inspector may simply record it as a two family house and ignore the attic, which may have been finished at a later point in time.)

WHAT TO LOOK FOR

A certificate of occupancy should be viewed with considerable care because it can, under some circumstances, show certain problems that might create difficulties later on for an owner or a mortgagee.

- A certificate of occupancy always specifies the type of use. What the type of use is will depend on the municipality, but typically, for a home, it might indicate residential use. In a multifamily dwelling, it may specify two-family house, three-family house, or something else. When someone is purchasing a multifamily dwelling (e.g., a two-family) the certificate of occupancy is the first clue as to whether the additional "tenant" in the basement is a legal tenant, or an illegal one. This has an important bearing on subsequent rights; under New York law, for example, a landlord for an illegal apartment does not have the right to evict tenants.

- Is it temporary or permanent? Under some circumstances, a temporary certificate of occupancy may be used. This occurs, for example, when the Board of Standards and Appeals of the City of New York, or the board of adjustment in another community, permits a premise to be used for a particular purpose for only a limited period, after which it reverts back to its old use. If temporary, additional effort may be needed to secure a permanent certificate of occupancy.

- When you undertake construction and obtain building permits, the actual use may not change, but the certificate of occupancy may have to be amended. This minor problem can cause a glitch in a mortgage loan if not cured in timely fashion.

CHANGING THE CERTIFICATE OF OCCUPANCY

Securing a change in the certificate of occupancy may require the services of an attorney who specializes in real estate. It often involves going before a zoning board of adjustment and occasionally an appellate board; it invariably involves use of the courts.

DANGERS

- You may be shown a certificate of occupancy. But, does it apply to the current buildings, or was it issued prior to them being constructed? (One way of ascertaining whether or not a building predates certificates of occupancy is to request a title company to locate a photocopy of one of the many surveys that "map" various buildings; this would show buildings on the survey that existed prior to a certain point in time.)
- Detached garages can pose special problems. If a premises has a detached garage, a separate certificate of occupancy almost always is required. If it is not available, the purchaser of the premises could be required (if the garage is illegal) to take corrective action by the building department. The building department, especially if the garage is an older one, might recognize that it is impossible to bring the existing structure up to present code; in this case, the building department would direct that the structure be torn down.
- Some cities require an inspection upon the sale of any residential property. City inspectors from the building and safety department then check out the building for any illegal construction work such as the addition of an extra bathroom or new lighting. If original permits and plans have been lost, as sometimes happens, a C.O. from a particular date may be the

only way of convincing the city agency not to require the work be brought up to current code standards.

COMPARING THE C.O. WITH A SURVEY

Sometimes, a certificate of occupancy will show a garage, or other structure as will the survey and the survey reading. However, a survey *inspection* will reveal that the dimensions on the garage have been changed (i.e., that it has been enlarged). In such an event, typically, the certificate of occupancy should have been properly amended. Sometimes it is relatively simple to do so: The owner of the parcel need only go to the building department, obtain a permit, an inspection thereafter, and an amendment to the certificate. If an amendment is not obtained, the subsequent owners (assuming the sale is consummated) may find themselves in the position of being ordered to tear down the structure or to apply for a permit, and inspection. The building inspector is not obliged to utilize the code provisions in force at the time that the structure was erected, but rather the then-current codes, which may require expenditure of a substantial amount of money and effort in bringing the building up to code.

WHERE TO FIND THE CERTIFICATE OF OCCUPANCY

Information concerning the certificate of occupancy is never found in the title insurance policy itself, but only in the certificate and report of title. You can order it from your local municipal building department. It is important to note that some municipalities do not issue certificates of occupancy and, indeed, do not even issue building permits. If none was issued, a file should always be endorsed with a letter from the municipality indicating that it does not require a certificate of occupancy, or that if it does, none has been issued because the premises predates the ordinance.

PRECAUTIONS

- Because the certificate of occupancy is never actually found listed in the certificate of title insurance, property is often sold subject to the certificate of occupancy, subject to a survey, subject to a survey reading and a survey inspection, and that which would be reasonably disclosed by any of them individually, or when used together.

 Before you buy a new home, or a resale, be certain to order the certificate of occupancy from the building office. Check what is found against what is being offered for sale. There may be permits that were obtained to do electrical rewiring that was never finally inspected.

 That could cause problems later on when it comes time to resell. By examining it, you can get the seller to handle the necessary sign-offs before it becomes your problem. The resale will save you lots of time—and some money—in future legal costs.

Chapter 38

What Do I Need to Take to the Closing?

You are about to make the most significant economic investment of your life. Certainly, it is more money in one place than you would ever otherwise expect to invest. And now it's come to a head. It's all down to one event, the "closing." You've got a mortgage company or bank to satisfy, a title company with various requirements designed to permit you to take the premises lien free (except for the new mortgage), and a seller who expects you to comply with a purchase agreement.

The only trouble is the paralegal in your lawyer's office has not yet returned your telephone call to answer your compelling question: What do I need to do to expedite the closing? What should I bring with me to close escrow?

We'll get to the checklist in a moment, but first a word about whether you should go to the closing alone, or accompanied. If you have completed real estate transactions before and are savvy as to what different things mean, you can probably handle it. If not, be sure your attorney is present. You will have many questions and you cannot rely on the escrow officer or the real estate agent to explain them.

(Today, in some parts of the country, agents refuse to attend closings because they fear they will be asked legal opinions, which they may not render. When they do attend, it is typically as a broker, to collect their commissions.)

Every real estate closing has some differences, yet they all have many similarities. Here is a handy checklist of things you need to do (or have done on your behalf) before you are ready to close on your purchase of a lifetime.

- Your insurance broker can arrange for a homeowner's insurance policy, naming yourself (and spouse or other purchasers) as loss payee, and adding the name of the mortgagee, as their interest may appear. If you don't have the name of a broker, ask the agent who was involved in showing you the house. They'll usually be happy to make an introduction.

166

In some states, such as California, obtaining insurance has become very difficult because of heavy losses sustained by natural disasters such as earthquakes or hurricanes. Be sure to apply for insurance as soon as you have a purchase contract in hand and be sure the agent will honor the insurance policy for the 30 to 90 days it may take to close escrow. In some cases finding insurance may be the single hardest part of putting the deal together.

 If it's tough in your area to get insurance, be sure that your contract of sale has as a contingency that you can cancel the contract if insurance is not available at standard commercial or residential rates.

- When you find a policy, get a paid receipt for the premium (unless it is to be paid out of escrow), and get an original copy of the policy. You'll also need an original policy for the mortgagee (though this sometimes can be sent, later). Set the effective date as of the date of the tentative closing. Give yourself enough time; some companies can take a couple of weeks to provide the original of a policy of insurance.

- Call the real estate broker and arrange for a final walk-through to make certain that there is only "reasonable wear and tear" since you last saw the house, and not major damage.

- Review the title report to ascertain any special requirements that are asked for. Your lawyer (if you have one) should do this for you; but for some of it, particularly if you have been through it before, you can save time by doing it yourself. Typically, this may includes an affidavit of identity (asking what other name you may have been known by during the past 10 or 20 years). The reason for this is that a search will be conducted under that name for any judgments against you.

- If you're selling, you should clean up old and unpaid parking tickets that you may have; they may have matured to judgment, and formed a lien on the property. Clear title cannot be passed until these have been removed (paid).

- Be prepared to provide a marital history. In some states, a spouse has community property rights, and in others, equitable distribution. If you're purchasing a residence while married to someone—even if the spouse does not join in the transaction, or even if you're doing it to separate—it may create legal rights that constitute a title insurance headache later on. The title company will guide you on this.

- Check with your mortgage funding company to be certain that your commitment is still valid. It's amazing how many commitments expire without the borrower remembering it. Be sure that your lock-in of the interest rate is still valid.

- Be certain that you have enough money in your savings or checking account to provide certified or other good funds at the closing. Do not leave it for the last minute, because even if funds are deposited, the bank can require delays while waiting for the funds to be cleared. In any real estate closing, even one for the purchase of a modest residence, the closing costs inevitably end up higher than you think they will be. A good rule of thumb is to anticipate between $3,000 and $5,000 in closing costs before considering any extraordinary items such as purchase of personal property (refrigerator, furniture, etc.), or requirements under the contract for the absorption of some expenses, or even points.

TYPICAL CLOSING EXPENSES

- City taxes, town taxes, county taxes, either as an adjustment for those prepaid by the seller, or as a "pick up" by your new mortgage company.
- Assessments, payable over a period of years, including sidewalk repairs, road access or repair taxes, and similar expenses that you and some of your neighbors may share.
- Balance of application fee (if any) due your mortgage company.
- Loan origination fee; loan discount fee (if any).
- Appraisal fee.
- Credit report.
- Inspection fee.
- Tax service fee.
- Buydown fee.
- Veteran's Administration or lender's funding fee.
- Document Preparation Fee.
- Underwriting fee.

- Flood certification fee.

- Lender's attorney review fee.

- Third-party mortgage services fee.

- Closing fee.

- Processing fees paid by lender.

- Notice of settlement, postage, other mailing costs.

- Items required by lender to be paid in advance, which can include interest, taxes, insurance, and similar items.

- A credit report (usually cost about $50), required by most lenders.

- Fee for a survey endorsement read into the title report (usually fee is between $25 and $300).

- Fee for a new survey if no survey is locatable, or too old to satisfy lender's requirements (fees range from approximately $300 to $1,000 or more).

- Lender's title insurance (required by every bank, Fannie Mae lender, and others) depends on the amount of insurance, based on the purchase price. This will vary from transaction to transaction, but can be anywhere from $300 to $3,500, depending on the purchase price.

- Simultaneous fee policy which is your title insurance (confirm it with the bank) and is available at a lower reduced rate based on a sharing of the risk. Generally, a simultaneous fee policy is available at prices ranging from a nominal cost to about half the cost of the bank's policy.

- Homeowner's Insurance—most banks require that the first year be paid in advance.

 If you're buying and the seller has prepaid the taxes on the parcel, one of your closing costs will be to reimburse them for the portion that they paid, but not yet used. For example, if they pay second quarter taxes, and you closed on June 20, you owe them for 10 days' worth of taxes (June 20 through June 30). Be certain that you adjust on the basis of a 365-day year, instead of the 360-day year that is commonly used (an arcane practice that predates easy availability of calculators and computers). The difference is modest, but will carry forward to every item on your closing list.

If your mortgage has an impound account, chances are the lender will require a "pick-up" closing of the portion of taxes that will become due. Nearly every impound account permits the lender to collect $\frac{1}{12}$ of the annual taxes each month. Lenders like to have a modest reserve so that they can assure, a month before the taxes are due, that sufficient funds will be available to pay them. If you closed on June 20, for example, the next quarter's taxes are due July 1 (typically); it is thus expected that you pay those up front, as an additional closing cost, and perhaps an additional month for the bank to start the impound account taxes for the next quarter (third quarter). If you're able to pay the taxes yourself, and avoid the impound account, it may be a better deal—you get the use of the money until payment is due. If your taxes are $7,000 annually, that can mean $350 in your pocket.

 Mortgage recording fees vary from jurisdiction to jurisdiction. In New York, figure about 2 percent of your loan will go to this. If it is possible to assume an existing loan, or to take a mortgage by assignment, you will save plenty on the mortgage recording. You pay a tax on the fresh money, but no tax on the assigned mortgage balance. Even in jurisdictions that do not tax this, fees are charged for recording all instruments.

Be certain that you bring your checkbook to the closing, and that you have a reasonable balance for drawing last-minute checks. If your house has oil heat, for example, you'll adjust at the closing for the amount of oil in the tank that has already been paid for.

Anticipate that there will be unexpected closing costs that you just didn't think would crop up. They almost always do.

After the closing, you should get a closing statement from your lawyer, or from the title company. Keep it, if you're the buyer, together with the recorded deed (when it arrives) and the title insurance policy in a safe place. You'll need these documents again at a later point in time.

Improving the Property

Chapter 39

What Are Zoning Laws and How Can They Be Appealed?

Zoning is a legal limitation, created by a legislature or municipal authority, designed to place similarly used properties in proximity with other like properties. Usually, it is part of a master plan designed to obtain the highest, and best use, of land. It permits, or denies, the use of property in a particular manner, and may allow, or prohibit, the building of certain types of structures.

Originally, before government got involved in the process of zoning or restricting the uses of property, landowners sometimes did it for themselves with a series of restrictive covenants or deed restrictions that prohibited various uses. For example, many old deeds specifically prohibit the purchaser (as well as his heirs, successors, or assigns) from maintaining commercial stables on their property (too odoriferous), or from manufacturing vitriol products (too noxious) or even from erecting structures of any kind in their backyards so as to preserve the "open look" of the community.

Today, many communities have both a master plan and zoning laws. Permission to vary the law for a particular piece of property—seeking a variance—is commonplace. Zoning boards—sometimes called the "Board of Standards and Appeals" (New York City) or the "Board of Adjustment" (Fair Lawn, New Jersey), and by other names elsewhere—adjudicate various zoning issues.

TYPES OF ZONING CHANGES

Among the zoning changes that can be sought from a zoning board are:

- *Use Variance.* This appears to change the way in which real property is used. For example, if someone buys an old house with a barn and wants to change the barn into either a car garage or an art studio, a variance for the use would probably be required.

- *Setback.* This refers to the distance from the property line to buildings on real property. If your community requires 20 feet from each house to the edge of the property on the side yard, and you want to build on an extension as a family room, if the design comes, say, to within 18 feet of the property line, a variance is required—permission to build it that way. If permission is denied, you must conform to the zoning requirements.

- *Landscaping.* Most zoning laws have requirements for greenery or other improvements. This is typically called site plan work.

- *Ingress and Egress from a Property.* This can range from a driveway to a road. Zoning boards can be required to pass on a request to widen a home's driveway, too, if it deviates from the accepted norms for size.

- *Height Variance.* If your community allows houses of no more than two stories, and you want to build a three-story house, it's to the zoning board that you go. Is there a real height difference in that last half-story? Maybe not, but the zoning laws require permission, anyway.

- *Zone Change.* An owner may need to change the zone for a property from one classification to another: from rural agricultural to highway business, or from residential to neighborhood business, or from one type of residential use (perhaps a one-family house) to another (a two-family house).

- Approve a change based on a prior nonconforming use to the property.

VARIANCES

Here you want a change in the zoning just for your property. Initially, a municipality's building officer or construction official is the typical starting point in any zoning determination. You must show proposed building plans or changes to the property to the construction official who can grant a permit, or deny it. If it is denied (because the official believes that it deviates from the administrative zoning code), your next step is an appeal to the zoning board.

It's worthwhile visiting your local construction official to see if there isn't some basis to obtain the relief that you need, or, if there isn't, how to minimize the zoning variances that you need. Complicated variances may require legal assistance, and expert witnesses—both costly—which you want to avoid when possible. Once a decision is made to seek a variance from the existing zoning laws, the local state statute concerning zoning appeals comes into play. It varies from state to state, but there are some general guidelines as to what basis can be used to grant variances.

GENERAL GUIDELINES FOR GRANTING VARIANCES

Helpful Hint   It's a minor change such as the typical homeowner's appeal from the decision of an administrative officer (the construction official), which seeks additional living space for a few feet here or there.

Helpful Hint   Variance relief on the basis of hardship.

Helpful Hint   Variance relief on the basis of substantial benefit to the community or parcel of land.

Helpful Hint   Change in use of the property (either based on applicant's agreement to make certain changes or improvements, or for a limited period).

Helpful Hint   Nonconforming use change. Sometimes a property's zone has been changed (e.g., from one type of residential to another, or even from farmland to residential), and at a later point in time an addition or change or modification is proposed. It might now be allowed (because the authorized use is now different) and makes sense because it goes with the property, anyway (e.g., a porch that the owner wants to screen in and winterize).

Zoning, then, is usually part of a master plan. Every request—no matter how small—to a zoning board asks for a variance, or permission to deviate from the law. Board members (usually drawn from the community) understand this, and apply a set of general rules and guidelines before determining whether to approve the change or not (see Chapter 41 on how to present a case to a zoning board on your own). They may permit the change in whole, or in part, or they may deny it. In essence, they act as an appellate authority for the construction or building official, but the actions of the zoning board may also usually be appealed, either to a higher municipal authority (such as a borough or city council) or to the courts.

 If you're a homeowner seeking a minor variance, you may be able to handle the proceeding by yourself, saving considerable attorney's fees and expert fees.

Chapter 40

How Do I Object to a Proposed Zoning Change or Variance Request?

Not in my backyard! That's the rallying cry of many individuals who have received a notice (usually by mail) about a proposed plan to build something in close proximity to where they live. Not every variance—even by a homeowner seeking something modest—will be approved by a local zoning board. This is particularly true when there is a serious objection by a neighbor who has good reason—not simply a grudge match. Zoning boards constantly must consider on one hand the claimed needs of the applicant and measure on the other the needs of the neighborhood and the community as a whole. To even get to the consideration, however, there must be an objector.

WHAT TO DO

When you receive notice of the proposed change, you will probably not have seen the entire application. It is important that you take the time, before attending the hearing, to review the application for its accuracy and intent. You may find that your concerns aren't real, or that with a minor modification, the problem can be resolved.

Helpful Hint We can live without our friends, but not without our neighbors. Ask your neighbor if there's some way to resolve your concerns without going before the zoning board. Happy neighbors facilitate good zoning decisions.

Helpful Hint If the zoning board has a work session for discussing applications or theoretical problems, it is useful to attend and get a sense of what they think about the proposed change.

HOW TO OBJECT TO A PROPOSED VARIANCE

- Use index cards to make your points. Write down each point on a separate card. You can eliminate points easily that way—especially if they repeat what other neighbors have said. You can also easily change the order, to respond to the board's comments.

- Summarize your position on one index card. Let the summary take no more than a minute or two to deliver. Shorter is better. If you oppose only a small part of the application, say so.

 Less is sometimes more. If a case is going to be litigated, a transcript usually has to be ordered of the proceedings. The less said by you that is extraneous, the lower your cost will be when it comes time to pay for that transcript.

- Board members have listened to hundreds of objectors during the course of their service and don't need to hear your opinion about good zoning or planning or how variances violate the law and should therefore not be granted.

- Concentrate on the facts.

- Be prepared! Have your statements, your witnesses, your experts, and your questions ready to go.

- If you think that approval of the variance will damage property values, ask for the opinion of a local real estate agent. If this professional agrees with your assessment, ask if he or she will testify for you as an expert witness. It can be very effective, and an inexpensive way to help prove your case with an objective witness.

 Local realtors, if asked, will sometimes volunteer their testimony, at no cost, hoping for future referrals of business. Don't be afraid to ask. The board will usually recognize them as an expert in the real estate field, saving you a substantial expert witness fee.

- If you have photographs, bring more than one set so that you can keep a copy and have the other introduced into evidence (which the board members can look at).

Lay out your photographs on an 8½-by-11-inch piece of white paper, putting several on a page (four or six will usually fit, depending on size). Then have the page copied at a local color copier center, such as Kinko's (found across the United States). If the cost to reproduce color is $1 per page, it's still a lot cheaper, though not usually as good, than ordering multiple reprints of photos.

- Petitions signed by neighbors aren't usually welcomed by a board. A petition can't be cross-examined. You can be, and probably will be, if you object.

- If your objection is that the building is going to take up too much of the parcel and that there won't be much grass left, say so. Many boards are sympathetic to those who want a green community.

- If the zoning change sought would block light going into your property, say so. The original zoning laws in New York of 1916 were designed to prevent a loss of light, and most zoning boards are conscious of this.

- If your objections are not based on facts, but on opinions, you may wish to consider having expert testimony as part of your objection. Objectors can call witnesses the same as a proponent can.

- If you have environmental concerns, express them. More and more zoning boards are concerned with ground coverage and impervious surfaces that deny the groundwater the ability to be renewed. If there are possible hazardous materials, bring it to the board's attention.

- If there is a similar property in the neighborhood (or even in a neighboring community) that looks like the variance being sought, photograph it and show it to the board. Because it has already been done doesn't mean it can, or should, be done again. A picture can be worth a thousand words of testimony.

- Be brief. Be succinct. Don't be repetitive. Remember that when President Bill Clinton, then governor of Arkansas, was asked to place Governor Dukakis's name in nomination for the presidency in 1988, the biggest round of applause at the Democratic National Convention came when his long-winded speech wound down and he uttered the line "In conclusion. . . ." Don't let that happen to you.

Opposing a zoning variance is not that difficult, even if you're not a lawyer. It will require patience and, more likely than not, several appearances on different days before the zoning board. This is typical. Some boards have accelerated calendars for uncontested, noncontroversial matters. Others take matters in the order in which they come. Go with the flow.

THE PROCEDURE

When the chairman of the board or the board secretary asks whether or not there is any opposition, you should either stand, raise your hand, or do both and wait until you are recognized, then make your way to the front of the room. You should then read from your note card a brief statement as to why you are opposed, being careful to give your reasons succinctly, and without being argumentative. It's permissible to say (but only once) that the approval of the application would be bad zoning—but be prepared to tell the board why you think so. Less is really more. Plan for a short presentation to the board and be prepared to answer questions. Reserve the right to rebut the balance of the proponent's case, and reserve the right to summarize or conclude at a later point in time. With practice, and patience, it is entirely possible that you will succeed in either blocking, or modifying, the variance request that you so dislike.

Chapter 41

Can I Present My Own Case for a Variance to the Zoning Board?

Yes. It's done successfully all the time. In making a personal appearance before a zoning board to plead your own case for a minor variance or exception to the zoning ordinance, you must be a can-do person. You need to take a position, stake it out, and not be wobbly about it—though you must have a willingness to compromise for the benefit of the brief relationship you will have while wooing the local board. The following section identifies areas where it is probably safe for you to prepare your own case (or petition to the zoning board) and then to make your own presentation. Complicated cases, especially commercial cases, are probably best handled by those who are skilled in practicing before your local board.

TYPICAL CASES HANDLED BY INDIVIDUAL OWNERS

- Placing an add-a-level on your existing dwelling, which means that it follows the exact footprint of the house (unless your local ordinance prohibits second stories or has a height restriction that is strictly followed).

- Changing the height of a fence because of special circumstances concerning your property. A number of boards try to prevent a Fort Apache look in the neighborhood, so be prepared to compromise. But there may be special circumstances that will allow such a request to be granted. Disliking your neighbors isn't a good reason.

- Making your driveway wide enough to fit two cars, rather than the present one.

- Building a deck in the rear of your property.

- Making minor changes to a house, such as enclosing a sun room, enclosing a porch for more living space, removing an unsightly accessory building (such as a shed) and replacing it with a more modern structure.

- Undertaking small landscaping additions.
- Putting in a swimming pool.
- Altering your property to make it look more like other properties in the neighborhood.
- Improving your property to upgrade its use.
- Undertaking most minor site-plan items.
- Constructing an addition or instituting changes costing less than a modest sum, say $5,000.
- Making interior alterations that require a variance under your local ordinance, where the use is not being changed.

ADDRESSING THE ZONING BOARD

Most local zoning boards have citizen members, which is to say that your neighbors may be board members. They usually have a good sense of what is appropriate, or inappropriate, in an area; because they are neighbors they also want good zoning for the community. Zoning boards are bound by state statutes, as well as their own municipal land use ordinances. Most boards have a natural leniency for homeowners doing routine home improvement work such as expanding a kitchen, adding a bathroom, or gaining more living space by adding a level to a residence. They may have more resistance when it comes to encroaching on backyard greenery—or building that reaches into a side yard setback. There are no true and fast rules for how a homeowner or person with a small business can proceed; but, here is some advice that is worth considering if you are thinking about proceeding on your own before the zoning board:

Helpful Hint Talk to the local zoning officer and try and get a sense from him or her as to what the board's usual position is on requests like yours. Many zoning officers will be candid—even if they cannot predict how the board will actually vote on your request. They may tell you that in their experience, no one who ever tried to obtain a variance like yours has succeeded. Or, they may tell you that nearly every application succeeds if it is modified a certain way.

Helpful Hint See if other premises in your community have the addition or change, or "look" that you are trying to achieve. Then ask the local zoning official to show you the file on that parcel, to ascertain whether it was built that way or a variance was obtained. The fact that a variance was granted doesn't mean that yours will be, too; every parcel of land and each set of facts are different. But you can get a good sense of what the original application was, how it was changed, and what the board was willing to grant.

 If you're making a major addition, it may pay to ask your local architect for an opinion as to the zoning implications. Architects usually know the local board well and frequently appear before them. They may have to do so on your case, even if it is a homeowner's application. Their expert testimony can help make or break your case. If you get a thumbs-down, you certainly can proceed—but you might save the filing fee and expert's time by listening to the architect's advice.

Helpful Hint Sit in on a board meeting, including a "work session" if they have one. It will give you a really good sense of the type of cases that the board handles, their views on certain issues, and how they might decide the case that your papers will present.

 Don't be afraid to pay for an hour's worth of consultation with a local planning consultant or a local attorney specializing in land use law. This professional may be able to give you special pointers that will assist you before your local board.

Helpful Hint Read your local zoning law to see what its basic goals are, and try to prepare your case so it will meet those basic goals. After all, you are asking for an exception to the zoning ordinance; your variance literally runs contrary to the law of your community. But it can be granted if you present your case the right way.

Helpful Hint When your case comes up on the calendar, be prepared.

Helpful Hint On the day your case is called, be certain that any witnesses you intend to use are present (or if your board will allow brief adjournments, have the witnesses available on call so they can come over quickly and not interrupt the flow of the calendar).

Helpful Hint   Organize your presentation on index cards with one major point on each card. That way, you can alter the presentation easily if the board asks questions, or if it becomes apparent that you do not need to make a point you thought would be necessary.

Helpful Hint   Always be respectful of the members of the zoning board. They are almost always volunteers. Abusive language or argumentative conduct is counterproductive to your goal.

Helpful Hint   One index card should summarize the relief that you seek from the zoning board ("I am requesting that the board permit me to add a second (third) level to my present home, following its existing footprint").

Helpful Hint   One index card should summarize the reason or reasons you are making the request. ("The added level will give me more living space. It will give us four bedrooms instead of the two that we have now, and allow my family to eat in the kitchen, instead of the hallway.")

Helpful Hint   If a number of your neighbors have similar additions or changes, say so; if you are planning an addition that keeps the sight line with other properties, so that they are the same, mention that, too.

Helpful Hint   Be brief in your presentation to the board.

Helpful Hint   Be responsive to any inquiries made by board members, or counsel, or professional staff. Do not be argumentative in your response.

Helpful Hint   If you need more time to formulate an answer, or simply don't know, don't be afraid to ask for an adjournment—a postponement to another date—so that you can find the answer. With good preparation, not only can you prepare your case before the local zoning board, you can get your variance.

Chapter 42

Can I Cut the Branches off My Neighbor's Tree?

Not a recommended course of action without giving careful consideration to making certain that you only prune on your own property and cause no damage to the tree itself. Failure to follow this guideline could be a costly experience. "I think that I shall never see/A poem as lovely as a tree" is the way that poet Joyce Kilmer put it, shortly before he was killed in the trenches of World War I.

The law generally recognizes that the poem speaks true, and those who cut timber generally find that they have violated a statute that can result in treble damages, and attorney's fees; a very costly lyric, indeed. But, it usually doesn't cover circumstances where tree branches go over onto your land.

It may, on the other hand, cover those instances where the root of a tree (such as a maple) crosses boundaries and results in destruction of your land. In each instance, under common-law principles, the owners of the land burdened by the tree were entitled to cut off invading tree roots by exercising self-help. The reason: The law recognizes it as a "nuisance." There is a common-law right of self-help to lop off overhanging branches to the property line but no further. The same applies to the cutting of roots, provided that it doesn't cause extensive damage to the tree.

GENERAL RULES TO FOLLOW

- Overhanging tree branches may constitute a nuisance for which an action for damages lies.

- A nuisance like a trespass on land is an injury to the possession and creates a right of action in favor of the occupant.

- The person over whose land a tree's branches spread is entitled to his or her action for damages against the person who is responsible for their presence.

- The right of action depends on the fact that the trees overhang the adjacent landowner's premises, not on the character of the trees, that being merely an element in determining the amount of the damage sustained by reason of the nuisance.

WHAT TO DO

Actually, the best thing to do in this instance is to telephone your neighbor and ask him or her to cut down the nuisance. If the neighbor refuses, you can follow up with a written letter, advising him or her that your property is being subjected to an unwanted burden, and that you wish it removed. Failure of your neighbor to fix this would give you the right to bring a claim against your neighbor—which you could do in a small claims court or the superior court with the lowest monetary jurisdiction in your town.

 If you need a sample letter, and don't want to consult with a lawyer, the following could be used (tailored to the circumstances of the particular facts of your case).
    You should send the letter by certified mail, return receipt requested (being sure that you keep a copy for your records):

Dear Neighbor,

The trees that are on the westerly side of your property have their branches over a portion of my property. The leaves are blowing on our lawn, which we have to pick up, and the shade created has damaged the ability of our flowers to grow, and of us to enjoy sunshine. I would appreciate it if you would promptly prune them back to the lot lines at your own expense. If you do not do so within the next seven days, I will have the nuisance removed at your expense and seek to hold you liable for our damages. If it is necessary to utilize our property for the pruning, we have no objection so long as it is during reasonable business hours, and not before 8 A.M. Thank you for your consideration.

Sincerely,

OTHER CONSIDERATIONS

Helpful Hint   Reported decisions have sustained or recognized a cause of action for damages for injury caused by tree roots from a tree or trees planted by the owner of adjoining property or his predecessor, *Forbus v. Knight,* 24 Wash. 2d 297, 163 P.2d 822 (Sup. Ct. 1945); *Ferrara v. Metz,* 49 Misc. 2d 531, 267 N.Y.S.2d 823 (N.Y. Sup. Ct. 1966); *Shevlin v. Johnston,* 56 Cal. App. 563, 205 Pac. 1087 (Calif. Dist. Ct. App. 1922). *Abbinett v. Fox,* 103 N.M. 80, 703 P.2d 177 (N.M. Ct. App. 1985), affirms a judgment for damages for injury caused by roots from a neighboring cottonwood tree upon a specific trial court finding of negligence in "permitting" the roots to cross onto plaintiff's property.

Helpful Hint   The Restatement of Torts draws a distinction between nuisances resulting from artificial and natural conditions of land. The former are actionable, *Restatement, Torts 2d* 839 (1979); the latter are not, *Restatement, Torts 2d* 840.

Helpful Hint   A tenant who lives at premises with such an overhang generally is not responsible in damages to a third person for maintaining and keeping in repair upon the demised premises a structure erected thereon by his landlord, prior to the commencement of his term, which operates to the nuisance of such third person. The owner, on the other hand, is probably responsible. In some communities, the local land use and zoning ordinances require that trees be properly pruned.

    Check with your local zoning officials, and if this is a remedy, you can ask that they contact your neighbor to have them conform to the law. That makes the town officials the bad guys, and not you as neighbor.

Condos and Co-Ops

Chapter 43

What Should I Watch Out for When Buying a Condominium?

A condo, like a co-op is common or shared interest real estate. You own the title ("fee simple" in the case of a condo, stock in the case of a co-op) to the "air space" your unit occupies. In a large building, this may mean that you own the equivalent of an apartment with other units above, below, and on all sides around you. In the case of a townhouse (technically a "Planned Unit Development or PUD), you also own the land on which your unit sits and the air space above (up to a few hundred feet).

All of these different types of developments share their common spaces: walkways, landscaping, parking, recreational facilities and so on. In short, you not only are buying a home but usually also are getting the right to use a lot of amenities. In a sense, you're buying into a lifestyle. While this appeals to many people, it also has drawbacks.

Lawsuits by individual homeowners against the homeowners' association (the group that represents all owners and sets rules) over real or imagined affronts have been all too common and have tied up such associations in legal wrangles and, as will be explained, can impair the ability of owners to resell their condo or co-op. In other cases, needed repairs and maintenance to common areas (such as reshingling a roof or repainting exterior walls) have been put off causing deterioration of the property. Here are some concerns to be aware of before buying into shared-interest real estate.

WHAT TO WATCH FOR

- Does the unit have adequate covenants, conditions, and restrictions? Covenants, conditions, and restrictions set the basic rules for use of the development such as minimum square footage, voting rights, size of board, and so on. Many older developments had covenants, conditions, and restrictions that only filled a page and left out much that was needed. Modern covenants, conditions, and restrictions can run to a hundred pages or more.

- Is the development separately incorporated? If not, you could be heading for a morass of legal problems.

- Are any lawsuits pending against the development (homeowners' association)? If you discover there are some, it could mean poor management. Further, if the association loses and the award is greater than the insurance, each homeowner could be responsible for the difference. (Some states, such as California, have passed laws exempting homeowners from deficiency payments, provided minimum amounts of insurance are kept.)

- Are there clear and reasonable architectural guidelines? These could be vital if you later want to remodel or add on.

- Is the association solvent? Check its financial statements. This is critical. Is there a comfortable bank balance, or is each month hand to mouth?

- Are there adequate reserves to handle maintenance, repairs, and emergencies? A rule of thumb is that 25 percent of the annual budget should be put away as reserves.

- Is the project old and in need of repairs? If so, you might be assessed in the future and your monthly dues could go up dramatically.

- If you're buying a new and not fully completed development, how are sales going? If they are slow, is there a chance the developer/builder could collapse leaving many uncompleted units and the existing owners with a real headache?

- Does the homeowners' association provide insurance against earthquakes, hurricanes, or tornadoes? You may need it to get a mortgage (either when you buy or for the next buyer when you resell), but not be able to get this insurance individually.

- What is the ratio of owners to tenants? If there are more than 25 percent tenants, you could have problems with noise and maintenance. Tenants, generally, do not take as good care of a place or are as respectful to it as owners. You could also have trouble reselling if the ratio of tenants to owners is too high.

 Look for shared interest properties that are older than three years but younger than ten. During the first three years, most problems (if any) with the building develop and are corrected. After 10 years, the dues are usually increased to pay for major maintenance.

When a developer has an unusually large number of units, resale may be difficult because lenders may shy away from making a loan. Concentration of investment capital is the reason usually cited.

You don't need an attorney to buy a condo or co-op. But you do need to be able to read and understand all the documents including the by-laws and the covenants, conditions, and restrictions. If you can't and don't have a knowledgeable friend who can, getting an attorney's opinion of the documents could be money well spent.

Chapter 44

How Do I Deal with a Homeowners' Association?

Your home is your castle, and property owners reign over all that they survey, rulers of the house—unless they happen to own a condo, townhouse, co-op or even some single-family residences where there is a homeowners' association.

These are set up to handle all of the common areas as well as police sometimes very strict bylaws and covenants, conditions, and restrictions on the title. If you have a homeowners' association chances are that you will eventually come into disagreement with it. It's almost inevitable that this will happen simply because of the arrangement: You're interested in your needs and wants, the homeowners' association looks out for the general good of the whole association. Sooner or later the two will come into conflict. Further, the board of directors that runs the homeowners' association is made up of members just like yourself. And sometimes personal quarrels, jealousies, and other self-interests will cloud debates and create unfair decisions.

HOW TO DEAL WITH THE BOARD

The homeowners' association is, for practical purposes, the board of directors. They will typically have weekly or bimonthly meetings and at that time will consider the concerns and problems of members. If you have a disagreement, you'll need to take it up with them or a general manager they may hire. Just remember that no matter what happens, they're your neighbors and friends. You don't want to make them into enemies, if you can avoid it.

- Put it in writing. You want the pool closed at 9:00 P.M. instead of 10:00 P.M. because it's near your unit and noisy. Or you want to keep your work truck in your parking place, even though the rules say no commercial vehicles allowed, or you want to place a "For Rent" sign in your window, though no signs are permitted, or the gardening crew has been tramping on your flower bed. Write an informal note to the manager of the homeowners' association explaining the problem and asking for the relief you want. Chances are, if it's a responsive homeowners' association, and you're not asking for a serious variance, that's all it will take.

- If your request is more difficult, for example, the rules on signs or vehicle parking are very strict, you may want to call the manager to verify policy and to determine the procedure to get a variance. This is typically an appearance before the board to argue your case.

- If you're going to appear before the board at a regularly scheduled meeting, be sure you ask to be scheduled on the agenda. This ensures that they will have time for you and will be prepared to listen. When it's your turn, stand up and as clearly and succinctly as possible, explain what you want to do, why you want to do it, and how it will benefit (or at least not hurt) other owners. Do *not* bring a lawyer with you at this time. If a lawyer is sitting with you, the board will inevitably interpret this as an attempt at coercion and may reject your request out of hand.

- If your request is reasonable, you have good reasons, and the board is fair-minded, it probably will be accepted. On the other hand, the board may have good reasons for rejecting it, which they will normally explain. You can accept these or not.

WHEN YOUR REQUEST IS DENIED

Sometimes a request that seems reasonable to you can be denied for what seem to be arbitrary or capricious reasons. For example, you live in an "adults only" community. But your grandchildren come to visit on weekends and you want them to use the pool. Since the pool is for adults only, they can't. So you request that they be allowed to use the pool on Saturday mornings for a few hours when nobody else is there. And, incredibly, the board denies your very reasonable request!

- Get an attorney to send a formal letter to the board asking them to reevaluate their decision. Make sure that the letter points out that the children are your guests and you have the right to take guests into the pool area (if in fact you do have that right).

The one rule conflicts with the other. Say that this is an important issue for you and you would like to have it settled amicably. It won't cost much to have an attorney simply draft the letter. If it's on an attorney's stationery, the board will get the meaning. You're serious enough to go to court over this. Now the board will consult with its manager and legal advisor. If you have a leg to stand on, they will probably capitulate because homeowners' associations hate lawsuits. They drain resources, take up lots of time, and produce hard feelings. On the other hand, the board may feel that your case is legally weak. Further, they may cling to a principle they want to uphold. They may refuse.

 You can appeal to the membership directly. If you have a lot of friends and they are sympathetic, you can get a petition together and appeal to the board. This is a powerful tool. The board is elected and when the electorate presents a petition demanding a particular action, the board usually goes along (else it could be voted out).

If the petition doesn't work or the board continues to reject your demand, then your last alternative is legal action. But be aware, this can be very costly. This is usually not the domain of small claims court. Rather, you will probably need a lawyer to draft a complaint and file it in superior court. It costs can be many thousands of dollars. Followed all the way through including a trial, it could cost tens of thousands of dollars. All of which is to say that sometimes it is cheaper and easier to acquiesce to the rules, no matter how arbitrary they may seem, than to fight them. Just write it off as one of the drawbacks to offset the many advantages of living in a shared ownership community.

 Try public pressure. It can yield an amazing result. The same can come from public embarrassment or ridicule, which often can achieve what negotiations, and even lawyers, cannot.

One of your authors was serving as a board member, for a homeowners' association when a homeowner requested that his driveway be plowed during the winter because he was too old and feeble to do it himself, and couldn't afford to hire others. The problem was that by doing so, the homeowners' association would set a precedent for plowing everyone's driveway. His request was denied. But at every board meeting, he would show up with cane in hand, walk feebly to the front, and then weakly describe his plight—how he couldn't get out for food or emergency vehicles couldn't get in unless the driveway was plowed. He seemed oblivious to the board's rationale for denying his request. He created such a pitiful sight that eventually those members in attendance took his side and demanded the board plow his driveway. It became a cause célèbre amongst the membership, and ultimately, the board had to give in.

Which is to say, when you don't want to pay a lawyer's fees and you're dealing with a public body, try public pressure—it can accomplish amazing things! (Lawyers often try the same tricks, publicizing something with the media, to achieve a result that they could not otherwise obtain in court.)

Chapter 45

Can I Get My Children into the Swimming Pool in a "No Child" Condo?

This is a tough one, for which there is no easy solution. But it may be possible to require the condominium to relax its policy, or face the consequences of an expensive lawsuit that they could well lose. Throughout this book, the authors have resisted the tendency to say "been there, done that," even when it has been applicable.

This one is "been there, didn't do that" because sometimes, neighborliness just precludes the threats and besides, you can usually sneak the kids in for a fast dip in the pool or quick use of the hot tub (which is usually where the real problem is). There are some other solutions and ways to approach the problem, however. If it is claimed that there are rules and regulations that preclude it, here are the first steps that you ought to take:

- Ask to see the rules, in writing.
- Note the date when the rule(s) went into effect.
- Ask to see a copy of the meeting of the board of directors of the Condominium Association and see whether they voted on the rules.
- Check to see whether a quorum of the directors was present at the time that the rules were adopted.

Many condominium associations operate fast and loose because their membership doesn't insist otherwise. But rules that have not been properly adopted cannot be enforced. Proper adoption includes proper notice before the board and (sometimes) the membership, and then a recorded vote by a quorum of the board (and sometimes the membership).

- Were the members notified of the change?
- If your condo association requires that rule changes be either posted or that members be notified, was this done?

- What rules weren't followed by the board? Do they bear on the ultimate determination to ban the children from the pool?
- Have they posted a sign to warn children, and the condo owners, of the ban?
- Is the conduct discriminatory on the basis of age, gender, race, or origin? If so, and if unreasonable, it may violate various federal statutes.

REMEDIES AVAILABLE

Certain remedies are available. For example, the Age Discrimination Act of 1975 (42 U.S.C. § 6101) may be used if your condo association has been built with the help of any governmental funding.

Helpful Hint   The Age Discrimination Act of 1975, as amended, is designed to prohibit discrimination on the basis of age in programs or activities receiving federal financial assistance. The act also permits federally assisted programs and activities, and recipients of federal funds, to continue to use certain age distinctions and factors other than age that meet the requirements of the act and these regulations.

Helpful Hint   Finding "federal" funds in a condo project may be easier than you think, especially in an age where many banks and other institutions with mortgages have unplanned federal involvement with Resolution Trust, FDIC, and other government agencies.

Helpful Hint   The regulations that are involved can be found in Volume 45 of the *Code of Federal Regulations,* part 90 (45 C.F.R. part 90) and are based on the original regulations published in Volume 49 of the *Federal Register,* page 49,629 published December 21, 1984.

Helpful Hint   Fighting the condo board will be a time-consuming project that may stretch out over several months, or even longer. Open a file to start, and be sure to keep a copy of each piece of correspondence in it, chronologically.

Here's a case where spending some money may make sense. See a lawyer and ask if he or she would be willing (for a fixed fee) to come to a homeowner's association board meeting, where you intend to raise the issue. Then, introduce the visitor to the board (who earlier authorized your appearance) as your lawyer. Rather than face an expensive legal challenge, the board may decide that valor doesn't require them to stand pat with an unreasonable decision.

Helpful Hint Sometimes reasonable exclusions can be made on the basis of age. For example, prohibiting a child under the age of 12 from swimming without supervision (in an otherwise unguarded pool) is discriminatory, but probably legal under any circumstances. You should make an initial inquiry to the various members of the board of directors, including the condo association president, as to whether there is such a regulation and why it exists.

If the reason is simply to allow the older residents permanent peace and quiet (an admirable goal), it may be sustainable if it was done properly. But most condo associations don't take the time to do things properly—and you can therefore nullify the purported regulation, and force them to do it the right way. And if that happens, you get a second bite at the apple, to defeat the regulation.

Helpful Hint Keep in mind that the condo association board is only representative of its membership. You can undertake action to vote them out of office and to change the regulations if you (and a majority of your neighbors) believe they are being unreasonable.

Helpful Hint Always consider negotiating with the condo board before things get too serious. Usually, good neighbors can work these things out. Especially when visitors are going to be involved.

Helpful Hint Some states have comparable regulations and if the condo association has a recreational facility that serves alcohol, there is probably a basis to proceed under either state or federal law to halt discrimination that prevents youths from fully enjoying the facility.

Landlord and Tenant

Chapter 46

How Do I Collect Rent from Tenants Who Moved without Paying?

An epitaph for Rebecca Bogess (August 1688) recites, "A house she hath . . . / The tenant ne'er shall pay for reparation . . . / Nor will the landlord ever raise her rent, / Or turn her out of doors for nonpayment . . . / To such a house who would not tenant be?"

Tenants who don't pay, and then try and skip out before the landlord can collect rent, or try and abuse their security are all too common.

As a landlord, can you stop it? Yes, you can. But, you have to be prepared to wage a small war to do so. At times, it may resemble a theater of the absurd. Almost all real estate owners—from the owner of a single-family residence who elects to rent, to the owner of a two-family house, down to the owners of the largest commercial office buildings—get the shivers when the word "landlord" is flashed before them, because they know that they are about to enter into a realm that is stranger than science fiction, oftentimes more weird than Ripley's *Believe It or Not,* and financially perilous to the uninitiated or the underinformed.

Though the minefield of landlord-tenant relationships must be treaded on carefully, once the tenant has left and "stuck" the landlord with the last month or two of rent, the final state of the relationship comes to the forefront. If the landlord has evicted the tenant, and this has caused the nonpayment, this is a consequence of the underlying action.

If the eviction proceeding didn't address the nonpayment, you may be precluded from asserting it separately. If, on the other hand, the tenant merely left and neglected paying a couple of months' rent, you have a remedy. Note that courts tend to be remarkably sympathetic, especially when a marginal person is faced with the loss of his or her apartment-residence because a color television set or a night on the town was more important than putting aside money for rent. For example, a tenant in at least one Utah city who fails to pay rent may face criminal sanctions. In New York City, however, a tenant may have the right to "inherit" the rent control apartment of a parent, using prices that are so outrageously low as to be laughable. (In tough economic times, with unemployment rising, the difficulty of securing residential dispossesses will markedly increase.)

CONSIDERATIONS

If your tenant is gone, here are a couple of considerations that you may wish to make before deciding what course of action will yield the best results.

- Determine what the limits are of small claims court in your jurisdiction. If the rent is covered, this is a great forum for expeditious, inexpensive handling.
- If your lease has an arbitration clause (see following section), you can demand arbitration of the dispute or the nonpayment.
- You can consult with a lawyer, or bring claim in the civil part of your superior court, designed to obtain what you are entitled to.
- If the tenant left because of poor financial health, there may be federal, state, or municipal agencies that will pay part or all of their rental payments to you.
- Check your rental application from the tenant to see what assets are identified there, and whether pursuing the matter makes economic sense.
- Make sure you have a forwarding address for the tenant.

PREVENTIVE MEASURES

The maxim that an ounce of prevention is worth a pound of cure should be a landlord's first rule. Here are some things to consider before you rent that can avoid big problems after you rent:

- When a tenant fails to pay, and a landlord immediately commences dispossess proceedings, how long does it generally take from the commencement until a sheriff physically evicts a tenant? If that time is two months, then that is the minimum that the landlord ought to consider for a security deposit in the first place. (Note: Some states limit the maximum amount of a security deposit.)

Here's a clause you may wish to consider adding to your lease: "Any controversy (except nonpayment) that arises out of the leasehold shall be settled exclusively by binding arbitration under the rules then obtaining of the American Arbitration Association. Nothing herein shall preclude the landlord from seeking judicial assistance to dispossess tenant for nonpayment of rent." If there is a dispute, you can save substantially on legal fees by using this approach. But be mindful that the AAA's fees are also substantial.

- Another worthwhile clause to consider: "Any nonpayment dispute may, at landlord's option, be subject to arbitration. The arbitration may award the prevailing party reasonable attorney's fees."

- Of course, you should prequalify a tenant before taking the person on so that you know you have assets to chase should circumstances warrant. To do this, be sure you get a Social Security number and permission to secure credit reports for each occupant at the time that you enter into the lease to facilitate getting a second credit report later on.

BEFORE GOING TO SMALL CLAIMS COURT

Don't overlook using small claims court as a means of collecting rent that may be due. It's underutilized for this purpose, it's a very smart choice for a landlord dealing with a tenant who left voluntarily. Before you do, however, consider:

- Many large city courts have a backlog of cases. It may take more time than it is worth to get the money. Usually, a call to the local court clerk's office (handling landlord-tenant matters) will yield an answer as to the backlog, and the anticipated time frame.

 Do a credit check on your tenant before you commence litigation over the issue of unpaid rent. If, at the end of the day, you spend time and effort and have nothing to show for it because your former tenant has no assets, it isn't a worthwhile endeavor.

- Don't wait a long time before you commence a legal proceeding. The more time that you wait, the more the tenant will believe that you have no claim—and have no incentive to pay. The law may also presume that if you don't act promptly, you have no basis to act. Be sure that you keep strong documentation.

 To succeed in your case, you'll need to show a completed rental/lease agreement, records of rent payments, and evidence that the tenant left breaking the agreement. Chances are you won't need a lawyer for any of this— being careful and attending to details should do the trick.

Chapter 47

What about Rent Control?

Rent control is a statutory regulation of the pricing of housing that is used in many large cities and municipalities. It limits the return that the landlord can obtain on a real estate investment and prevents free market pricing of living space.

The often-stated goal is to provide affordable housing to certain tenants. Actually, as the name implies, there is no limitation that the rents being controlled must be residential rents. But in fact, except during wartime, the only controlling that has been done has related to residential tenancies. Inevitably, the regulation of the freedom to contract for rental prices has been precipitated by an actual emergency.

World War II, for example, was noted for the imposition of rent controls in New York City and many other large municipalities throughout the nation. The imposition of the economic controls was also accompanied by wage and price controls and rationing of scarce goods (of which housing was one). If rationing's purpose was to allow all people an even chance to obtain food and necessities, then rent control's goal was to prevent rent scalping and to change the rules of the marketplace so that the scarce housing stock would not get auctioned to the highest bidder.

Well, a half century after the emergency that brought rent control to New York City, it is still being imposed in the name of that earlier crisis. Certain luxury apartments have been gradually exempted in the 1990s, and decontrolled so that they can achieve market rents, but for the most part, the Naked City that spawned Neil Simon's *2 Rms Rvr View,* a play about rent-controlled apartments, still has controls over hundreds of thousands of apartments.

In the name of providing low-cost housing to low-income families (particularly during inflationary times when rental rates rose rapidly), rent control has been imposed on many other communities across the United States over the past 50 years. In general, however, the reduction in economic return that rent control imposes has resulted in run-down housing and neighborhoods and as a consequence, it does not enjoy the favor it once did.

LEGALITY OF RENT CONTROL

Rent control has been tested in the courts, both at the time of imposition, and decades later, and each time the Supreme Court has held that it is within the inherent powers of the government to regulate this unique aspect of contract, even though government may not legally regulate other aspects of the contract without paying compensation to the property owner. Compelling arguments can, and have been made, that rent control is unconstitutional; that it is a taking of property without compensation or due process; that it is a violation of the right to contract. They have been unavailing in the courts. For the landlord in a city that imposes rent controls, as well as the tenant who seeks to utilize the controls to benefit from low rent, here are some handy points to consider about rent control properties. Remember, that rent control is not aimed at causing the downgrading of the housing stock, or eliminating landlord control over buildings, even though that may be an inevitable consequence:

- Nearly all rent control regulations permit owners to repossess a unit for their own use. This can result in dismissal of a long-term tenant. Tenants should exercise caution, therefore, in assuming that the controls are necessarily permanent.

- For tenants, residency at the premises under control—real residency—is essential. If it is a *pied-a-terre* (a secondary "in-town" apartment) you're likely to lose it and, in addition, have an expensive lawsuit.

- Tenants should read the lease that is involved carefully and see what it says about the control.

- Read the local rent control regulations and see precisely what they provide, and what they don't. What isn't provided for is sometimes more important than what the regulations do provide.

- Rent control statutes or regulations exist in about a third of the United States to varying degrees. Court challenges have occurred in the last dozen years in at least half of those jurisdictions.

- Know your landlord and know your tenant. Both are important in any rent control context.

- Violations of any material term of the tenancy can result in termination of the control or the regulation.

It seems unlikely that rent control regulations are likely to be terminated any time soon. The issue is too political—landlords may contribute money to political campaigns, but it is the tenants who actually vote. What this means as a practical matter is that rent control regulations continually are extended by the various legislative authorities that have the right to do so. As noted, in New York the 1945 emergency legislation was ratified in 1963 with a declaration that the same "emergency" was still in effect. (It has since been modified to allow for rent stabilization to handle apartments as they become decontrolled, but that decontrol is a very slow process.)

WHEN THERE IS A PROBLEM

When both the landlord and the tenant in a rent control jurisdiction, they are likely to be familiar with the landlord-tenant or housing court. This is simply an unfortunate fact of life. In preparing for the inevitable, it is useful to consider these historical aspects of rent control regulations, which affect how courts interpret existing law:

Helpful Hint Most rent control ordinances allow for a gradual increase in rent, sometimes set as a percentage of the rent (2 percent per year) or as a percentage of the rate of inflation.

Helpful Hint Many rent control ordinances provide that when a tenant voluntarily moves out, the landlord at that time may adjust the rent to the market price. But thereafter, the rent controls go back into force.

Helpful Hint Rent controls exist in California, Connecticut, Florida, Hawaii, Illinois, Maryland, Massachusetts, Missouri, New Jersey, New York, Ohio, Pennsylvania, Wisconsin, Washington, DC, and at some municipal levels elsewhere.

Helpful Hint Foreign rent control is even more intrusive than American law. In Italy, the Fair Rental Act of 1978 requires that residential leases be offered for a term of four or more years, and commercial leases for at least six years. The amount of rental is also fixed. France requires commercial leases to have a life of at least nine years. Quebec also has the Regie du Logement, created in 1979 to cover dwelling leases.

If you're a rent-controlled tenant, sometimes you can approach your landlord with a buyout offer. This means that you ask your landlord to buy you out of the lease for a fixed price. Sometimes, it's worth it for the landlord—and for you—to consider such a proposition. The amount that a landlord will pay is in proportion to the rate of return for a vacant apartment.

Real Estate Taxation

Chapter 48

What Are the "Rollover" Rules?

If you sell a home and invest the proceeds in another residence within four years (two years before or after the sale), provided you meet certain requirements, there are no taxes to pay immediately. Taxes are deferred.

There are two things in life that are a certainty: death and taxes. Avoiding taxes on large capital asset sales is a national preoccupation, but in the case of a home, there is a perfectly legitimate way to postpone the payment of taxes almost indefinitely.

 This technique (technically called "deferral of gain") is legal and can help put off your day of reckoning with the tax man for many years—at which time you may be able to minimize the gains tax that you will have to pay by using the $125,000 lifetime exemption (see Chapter 49).

Rules to accomplish this are not very complicated, though the accounting can be complex at another point in time; the key is sticking to the time frame—no more than two years before or after the date of sale. And to roll over the entire gain, the second house must cost more than the first. If it costs less, then only a portion of the gain may be rolled over.

BASIC REQUIREMENTS

- The residence sold must be the principal residence. That means your main house, the one in which you reside. A lot of variety is available here, however. It can be a single-family home, a condo, a houseboat or even a RV vehicle.
- The residence purchased must be your principal residence.
- If the cost of the new residence is more than or equal to the old residence, none of the gain is recognized.
- If the cost of the residence is less than the old residence, then only a portion of the gain may be recognized.

- You must sell one residence and buy another within four years (two before or two after) the date of the original sale. The date of the closing is what governs. If you exceed the limit, the gain is a capital gain, and taxes must be paid.

- If the second house is new construction, then you must actually occupy the property within the two-year limit.

- There are certain exceptions if you are in the military or if you are required to move as part of your job.

- You may only use the rollover once every two years. If you use it more often, you may have to pay capital gains tax on the "house in the middle."

- The house must be your principal residence. Just being residential property won't do. You can't use this rule on rental residential property. There are a number of other tax considerations that you need to carefully consider, and some caveats you should bear in mind as you contemplate this type of real estate transaction.

Helpful Hint   You do not have to put the money you get from the first house into the second. The trail of the proceeds does not actually have to go from one house to another. The test is simply whether or not you sold a principal residence and within two years purchased another principal residence.

Helpful Hint   The law merely delays payment of the tax; it does not eliminate it. At such time that you eventually sell the last property and do not reinvest in another principal residence (within the time limits), the gains over your cost (plus capital improvements) is a taxable capital gain. If, for example, over your lifetime you've gone through four principal residences, the gains that you rolled over from all four now, in effect, become taxed when you sell the last and then do not buy again, within the time limits.

Helpful Hint   If the government condemns the property that you live on, you are permitted to call this a "sale" for rollover purposes under Internal Revenue Code § 1034(i).

Helpful Hint   Ownership of stock in a cooperative housing corporation (a co-op) has been held to be the equivalent of the ownership of a residence. Trailers or houseboats are given the same role so long as a principal residence is involved.

Helpful Hint You do not have to reside in the house at the moment of sale; you can depart and rent out the old house before its sale, or even rent the new residence before consummating the transaction. Before the end of the two-year holding period, however, you must move into the new place and call it your residence. Also, it is not clear for how long you may rent out your old and still claim it as your principal residence. One rule of thumb that accountants have used is that if you rent it out for no more than two years, you'll probably be okay.

Helpful Hint Under Internal Revenue Code § 1034 and the regulations that the IRS has promulgated, only one residence can be used at a time.

Helpful Hint The rule is mandatory, not optional. You cannot elect not to defer, if you qualify under the rules.

In arriving at the sums involved in the calculations, it is essential to know the tax basis for the residence being sold, and for the residence being purchased. It is not enough that you originally paid $150,000 for one house, did $40,000 worth of work in it by adding a dormer, and then had to sell it for $160,000, only to then buy a house for $175,000. If you had made capital improvements—like adding a dormer for $40,000—you actually have a loss, and the new tax basis that you start with will be $175,000. Check with your accountant because the method used for determining "basis" and "gain" is precisely prescribed and must be followed to the letter. The "cost" of the new residence includes cash paid, and any indebtedness (mortgage) incurred. To the extent that a buyer acquires a portion of a residence by gift or inheritance, the Internal Revenue Code does not consider this to be a portion of the cost.

DO YOU NEED AN ATTORNEY?

Yes and no. You certainly need a competent accountant. Where there is some question about time frames or whether the property qualifies, you may also want a legal opinion.

Chapter 49

What Is the Once-in-a-Lifetime $125,000 Benefit and How Do I Get It?

If you own your house for at least three years, and have resided in it for the past three of the past five years, you may qualify when you or your spouse sell your home, if you are over age 55. Your home is not only your castle, but it is also your financial security blanket for the future in your golden years.

One of the few tax shelters left for the middle class is their personal residence. Congress changed the law a couple of years ago to allow retirees a healthy shot in the arm that would help them best plan for their postworking future. Actually, you do not have to be retired to take advantage of the plan, you just have to be over the age of 55.

If you are married, only one spouse has to be over the magical age barrier. Under the terms of the law, the key requirements, if met, qualify you to take advantage of price appreciation of real estate—and allow you to retain a substantial amount of gain without paying any federal income tax or capital gains tax on the appreciation:

- You or your spouse is age 55, or over.
- You have lived in the house for at least three of the previous five years.
- You have owned the property for at least three years.
- Profits, after expenses, from the sale are $125,000 or less. If the profits are more, only the first $125,000 are free; if the profits are less, only the amount of the profit up to $125,000 is tax free.
- You file an informational return with the IRS advising them you plan to take advantage of this program. The way this works is surprisingly simple. You simply calculate the gain on your home and up to the first $125,000 is yours to keep, tax free. There are some important caveats, and other considerations, that you may want to think about.

You can only use the lifetime exemption once. Make certain that you are maximizing it. If you sell a home at age 55 and don't get the full exemption, you can't later claim the portion you didn't receive. For example, your gain was only $75,000—you can't later claim the remaining $50,000 that was allowed.

Helpful Hint   If you buy another home, and use it for many more years, and believe that the value will appreciate even more, you might not want to consider selling it to take full lifetime exemption until later. There is no guarantee, of course, that Congress won't repeal it in the meantime.

Helpful Hint   Congress's actions in fact do not exempt you from payment of any state or municipal taxes that might be due by virtue of the sale.

If two unmarried parties have each made an independent election to marry each other, after each taking advantage of the lifetime exemption previously, there is no recapture of the tax previously excluded by either one.

Helpful Hint   You report the transaction on IRS Form 2119. Any gain not subject to the exemption goes on Schedule D, Form 1040.

Helpful Hint   The residence that you may sell includes a condominium or stock in a cooperative housing corporation, as well as a traditional house.

Helpful Hint   The property involved must be a principal residence—not a vacation house. For further information, see Internal Revenue Code § 121 and Treasury (Income Tax) Regulation § 1.121-1 *et seq.*

If there's an issue concerning a vacation home—perhaps it has appreciated in value while your current primary residence hasn't—you can take steps to make the vacation home your new primary residence, and after the appropriate time frame, sell it. There are a number of tests for residency, and you'll have to meet them before taking advantage of this distinctive provision of the tax law.

Taking advantage of the lifetime exemption should involve some planning. Certainly, it may involve some estate planning as well, since income removed this way eventually is taxed differently than the real property (which obtains a stepped-up basis under the Tax Code). But all in all, it affords virtually every American who owns his or her own residence—and who reaches the vaulted status of being 55—the ability to have a true tax shelter that isn't available to the population as a whole.

If you are thinking about moving, or retiring, you need to bring this into your overall financial plan, since it basically gives you up to a $125,000 tax-free gain—the equivalent of more than $30,000 tax dollars in your pocket for most people. That means there is the possibility of more income, and more importantly, more principal to draw on in your golden years.

DO YOU NEED AN ATTORNEY?

Yes and no. You certainly need a competent accountant. Where there is some question about time frames or whether you or the property qualifies, you may also want a legal opinion.

Appendix

Real Estate Forms

1 Residential Contract of Sale
2 Lease
3 Deed

ABOUT THE FORMS

This book focuses on issues that you're likely to encounter if you buy, sell, or rent a primary residence; invest in a small piece of commercial property; or want to supervise the building of your own home. However, a couple of words of warning are in order. A form is just that: something that is usable in the abstract, but that requires changes to adapt it to the real-world conditions, and to make certain that it accomplishes its goal of protecting you while creating a binding obligation or contract.

We're very lucky to have been able to draw on several sources for the forms in this book. Two legal stationers have granted us permission to reprint their forms in the Appendix. The firms of Julius Blumberg & Co., Inc., of New York City, and All State Legal Forms, of Cranford, New Jersey, have both been generous in permitting use of some of their real estate forms.

Both firms publish law blanks—forms that are filled in and added to—Blumberg for more than a century, All State for the past 50 years. Each firm has a fine editorial staff, some of whose work has helped the form of the Appendix to this book. Arthur McGuire, Esq., the general counsel to Blumberg, has graciously permitted us to reprint, in entirety, a widely used format for a contract of sale, and also a widely used apartment lease. (If you like the forms, you can obtain them by either writing or faxing Blumberg, or by inquiring at the many commercial stationers throughout the United States that carry the forms.) All State's forms are widely used in New Jersey, and elsewhere. A deed is included.

With both Blumberg or All State forms, we acknowledge their copyrights, and their generosity in allowing reproduction of the forms. If you use any of these forms yourself, please comply with the copyright laws and acquire the format from any commercial stationer, or from the manufacturer.

FORM 1

A 125—Residential contract of sale. 3-92

Blumberg Law Products

JULIUS BLUMBERG, INC.,
PUBLISHER, NYC 10013

Jointly prepared by the Real Property Section of the New York State Bar Association, the New York State Land Title Association, the Committee on Real Property Law of the Association of the Bar of the City of New York and the Committee on Real Property Law of the New York County Lawyers' Association.

WARNING: NO REPRESENTATION IS MADE THAT THIS FORM OF CONTRACT FOR THE SALE AND PURCHASE OF REAL ESTATE COMPLIES WITH SECTION 5-702 OF THE GENERAL OBLIGATIONS LAW ("PLAIN LANGUAGE").

CONSULT YOUR LAWYER BEFORE SIGNING THIS AGREEMENT

NOTE: FIRE AND CASUALTY LOSSES AND CONDEMNATION.
This contract form does not provide for what happens in the event of fire, or other casualty loss or condemnation before the title closing. Unless different provision is made in this contract, Section 5-1311 of the General Obligations Law will apply. One part of that law makes a Purchaser responsible for fire and casualty loss upon taking possession of the Premises before the title closing.

Residential Contract of Sale

Contract of Sale made as of   19   BETWEEN

Address:
Social Security Number/Fed. I. D. No(s):   hereinafter called "Seller" and

Address:
Social Security Number/Fed. I. D. No(s):   hereinafter called "Purchaser".

The parties hereby agree as follows:

1. Premises. Seller shall sell and convey and Purchaser shall purchase the property, together with all buildings and improvements thereon (collectively the "Premises"), more fully described on a separate page marked "Schedule A", annexed hereto and made a part hereof and also known as:

Street Address:

Tax Map Designation:

Together with Seller's ownership and rights, if any, to land lying in the bed of any street or highway, opened or proposed, adjoining the Premises to the center line thereof, including any right of Seller to any unpaid award by reason of any taking by condemnation and/or for any damage to the Premises by reason of change of grade of any street or highway. Seller shall deliver at no additional cost to Purchaser, at Closing (as hereinafter defined), or thereafter, on demand, any documents which Purchaser may reasonably require for the conveyance of such title and the assignment and collection of such award or damages.

2. Personal Property. This sale also includes all fixtures and articles of personal property now attached or appurtenant to the Premises, unless specifically excluded below. Seller represents and warrants that at Closing they will be paid for and owned by Seller, free and clear of all liens and encumbrances, except any existing mortgage to which this sale may be subject. They include, but are not limited to, plumbing, heating, lighting and cooking fixtures, bathroom and kitchen cabinets, mantels, door mirrors, switch plates and door hardware, venetian blinds, window treatments, shades, screens, awnings, storm windows, storm doors, window boxes, mail box, TV aerials, weather vane, flagpole, pumps, shrubbery, fencing, outdoor statuary, tool shed, dishwasher, washing machine, clothes dryer, garbage disposal unit, range, oven, refrigerator, freezer, air conditioning equipment and installations, wall to wall carpeting and built-ins not excluded below (*strike out inapplicable items*).

Excluded from this sale are furniture and household furnishings and

3. Purchase Price. The purchase price is '

                                    $
payable as follows:
 (a) on the signing of this contract, by Purchaser's check payable to the Escrowee (as hereinafter defined), subject to collection, the receipt of which is hereby acknowledged, to be held in escrow pursuant to paragraph 6 of this contract (the "Downpayment"):
                                    $
 (b) by allowance for the principal amount unpaid on the existing mortgage on the date hereof, payment of which Purchaser shall assume by joinder in the deed: $
 (c) by a purchase money note and mortgage from Purchaser to Seller: $
 (d) balance at Closing in accordance with paragraph 7: $

4. Existing Mortgage. (*Delete if inapplicable*) If this sale is subject to an existing mortgage as indicated in paragraph 3(b) above:
 (a) The Premises shall be conveyed subject to the continuing lien of the existing mortgage, which is presently payable, with

interest at the rate of   percent per annum, in monthly installments of $ which include principal, interest and escrow amounts, if any, and with any balance of principal being due and payable on
 (b) To the extent that any required payments are made on the existing mortgage between the date hereof and Closing which reduce the unpaid principal amount thereof below the amount shown in paragraph 3(b), the balance of the price payable at Closing under paragraph 3(d) shall be increased by the amount of the payments of principal. Seller represents and warrants that the amount shown in paragraph 3(b) is substantially correct and agrees that only payments required by the existing mortgage will be made between the date hereof and Closing.
 (c) If there is a mortgage escrow account, Seller shall assign it to Purchaser, if it can be assigned, and in that case Purchaser shall pay the amount in the escrow account to Seller at Closing.
 (d) Seller shall deliver to Purchaser at Closing a certificate dated not more than 30 days before Closing signed by the holder of the existing mortgage, in form for recording, certifying the amount of the unpaid principal, the date to which interest has been paid and the amounts, if any, claimed to be unpaid for principal and interest, itemizing the same. Seller shall pay the fees for recording such certificate. If the holder of the existing mortgage is a bank or other institution as defined in Section 274-a of the Real Property Law ("Institutional Lender"), it may, instead of the certificate, furnish a letter signed by a duly authorized officer, employee or agent, dated not more than 30 days before Closing, containing the same information.
 (e) Seller represents and warrants that (i) Seller has delivered to Purchaser true and complete copies of the existing mortgage, the note secured thereby and any extensions and modificatons thereof, (ii) the existing mortgage is not now, and at the time of Closing will not be, in default, and (iii) the existing mortgage does not contain any provision that permits the holder of the mortgage to require its immediate payment in full or to change any other term thereof by reason of the sale or conveyance of the Premises.

5. Purchase Money Mortgage. (*Delete if inapplicable*) If there is to be a purchase money mortgage as indicated in paragraph 3(c) above:
 (a) The purchase money note and mortgage shall be drawn by the attorney for Seller in the form attached or, if not, in the standard form adopted by the New York State Land Title Association. Purchaser shall pay at Closing the mortgage recording tax, recording fees and the attorney's fees in the amount of $ for its preparation.
 (b) The purchase money note and mortgage shall also provide that it is subject and subordinate to the lien of the existing mortgage and any extensions, modifications, replacements or consolidations of the existing mortgage, provided that (i) the interest rate thereof shall not be greater than   percent per annum and the total debt service thereunder shall not be greater than $ per annum, and (ii) if the principal amount thereof shall exceed the amount of principal owing and unpaid on the existing mortgage at the time of placing such new mortgage or consolidated mortgage, the excess be paid to the holder of such purchase money mortgage in reduction of the principal thereof. The purchase money mortgage shall also provide that such payment to the holder thereof shall not alter or affect the regular installments, if any, of principal payable thereunder and that the holder thereof will, on demand and without charge therefor, execute, acknowledge and deliver any agreement or agreements further to effectuate such subordination.

6. Downpayment in Escrow. (a) Seller's attorney ("Escrowee") shall hold the Downpayment for Seller's account in escrow in a segregated bank account at

until Closing or sooner termination of this contract and shall pay over or apply the Downpayment in accordance with the terms of this paragraph. Escrowee shall (*not*) (*Delete if inapplicable*) hold the Downpayment in an interest-bearing account for the benefit of

(CONTINUED)

the parties. If interest is held for the benefit of the parties, it shall be paid to the party entitled to the Downpayment and the party receiving the interest shall pay any income taxes thereon. If interest is not held for the benefit of the parties, the Downpayment shall be placed in an IOLA account or as otherwise permitted or required by law. The Social Security or Federal Identification numbers of the parties shall be furnished to Escrowee upon request. At Closing, the Downpayment shall be paid by Escrowee to Seller. If for any reason Closing does not occur and either party gives Notice (as defined in paragraph 25) to Escrowee demanding payment of the Downpayment, Escrowee shall give prompt Notice to the other party of such demand. If Escrowee does not receive Notice of objection from such other party to the proposed payment within 10 business days after the giving of such Notice, Escrowee is hereby authorized and directed to make such payment. If Escrowee does receive such Notice of objection within such 10 day period or if for any other reason Escrowee in good faith shall elect not to make such payment, Escrowee shall continue to hold such amount until otherwise directed by Notice from the parties to this contract or a final, nonappealable judgment, order or decree of a court. However, Escrowee shall have the right at any time to deposit the Downpayment and the interest thereon with the clerk of a court in the county in which the Premises are located and shall give Notice of such deposit to Seller and Purchaser. Upon such deposit or other disbursement in accordance with the terms of this paragraph, Escrowee shall be relieved and discharged of all further obligations and responsibilities hereunder.

(b) The parties acknowledge that, although Escrowee is holding the Downpayment for Seller's account, for all other purposes Escrowee is acting solely as a stakeholder at their request and for their convenience and that Escrowee shall not be liable to either party for any act or omission on its part unless taken or suffered in bad faith or in willful disregard of this contract or involving gross negligence on the part of Escrowee. Seller and Purchaser jointly and severally agree to defend, indemnify and hold Escrowee harmless from and against all costs, claims and expenses (including reasonable attorneys' fees) incurred in connection with the performance of Escrowee's duties hereunder, except with respect to actions or omissions taken or suffered by Escrowee in bad faith or in willful disregard of this contract or involving gross negligence on the part of Escrowee.

(c) Escrowee may act or refrain from acting in respect of any matter referred to herein in full reliance upon and with the advice of counsel which may be selected by it (including any member of its firm) and shall be fully protected in so acting or refraining from action upon the advice of such counsel.

(d) Escrowee acknowledges receipt of the Downpayment by check subject to collection and Escrowee's agreement to the provisions of this paragraph by signing in the place indicated on the signature page of this contract.

(e) Escrowee or any member of its firm shall be permitted to act as counsel for Seller in any dispute as to the disbursement of the Downpayment or any other dispute between the parties whether or not Escrowee is in possession of the Downpayment and continues to act as Escrowee.

7. Acceptable Funds. All money payable under this contract, unless otherwise specified, shall be paid by:

(a) Cash, but not over $1,000.00;

(b) Good certified check of Purchaser drawn on or official check issued by any bank, savings bank, trust company or savings and loan association having a banking office in the State of New York, unendorsed and payable to the order of Seller, or as Seller may otherwise direct upon not less than 3 business days notice (by telephone or otherwise) to Purchaser;

(c) As to money other than the purchase price payable to Seller at Closing, uncertified check of Purchaser up to the amount of $; and

(d) As otherwise agreed to in writing by Seller or Seller's attorney.

8. Mortgage Contingency. (*Delete if inapplicable*) The obligations of Purchaser hereunder are conditioned upon issuance on or before   , 19   , (the "Commitment Date") of a written commitment from any Institutional Lender pursuant to which such Institutional Lender agrees to make a first mortgage loan, other than a VA, FHA or other governmentally insured loan, to Purchaser, at Purchaser's sole cost and expense, of $ or such lesser sum as Purchaser shall be willing to accept, at the prevailing fixed rate of interest not to exceed   or initial adjustable rate of interest not to exceed   for a term of at least   years and on other customer commitment terms, whether or not conditional upon any factors other than an appraisal satisfactory to the Institutional Lender. Purchaser shall (a) make prompt application to an Institutional Lender for such mortgage loan, (b) furnish accurate and complete information regarding Purchaser and members of Purchaser's family, as required, (c) pay all fees, points and charges required in connection with such application and loan, (d) pursue such application with diligence, (e) cooperate in good faith with such Institutional Lender to obtain such commitment and (f) promptly give Notice to Seller of the name and address of each Institutional Lender to which Purchaser has made such application. Purchaser shall comply with all requirements of such commitment (or of any other commitment accepted by Purchaser) and shall furnish Seller with a copy thereof promptly after receipt thereof. If such commitment is not issued on or before the Commitment Date, then, unless Purchaser has accepted a commitment that does not comply with the requirements set forth above, Purchaser may cancel this contract by giving Notice to Seller within 5 business days after the Commitment Date, in which case this contract shall be deemed cancelled and thereafter neither party shall have any further rights against, or obligations or liabilities to, the other by reason of this contract, except that the Downpayment shall be promptly refunded to Purchaser and except as set forth in paragraph 27. If Purchaser fails to give notice of cancellation or if Purchaser shall accept a commitment that does not comply with the terms set forth above, then Purchaser shall be deemed to have waived Purchaser's right to cancel this contract and to receive a refund of the Downpayment by reason of the contingency contained in this paragraph.

9. Permitted Exceptions. The Premises are sold and shall be conveyed subject to:

(a) Zoning and subdivision laws and regulations, and landmark, historic or wetlands designation, provided that they are not violated by the existing buildings and improvements erected on the property or their use;

(b) Consents for the erection of any structures on, under or above any streets on which the Premises abut;

(c) Encroachments of stoops, areas, cellar steps, trim and cornices, if any, upon any street or highway;

(d) Real estate taxes that are a lien, but are not yet due and payable; and

(e) The other matters, if any, including a survey exception, set forth in a Rider attached.

10. Governmental Violations and Orders. (a) Seller shall comply with all notes or notices of violations of law or municipal ordinances, orders or requirements noted or issued as of the date hereof by any governmental department having authority as to lands, housing, buildings, fire, health, environmental and labor conditions affecting the Premises. The Premises shall be conveyed free of them at Closing. Seller shall furnish Purchaser with any authorizations necessary to make the searches that could disclose these matters.

(b) (*Delete if inapplicable*) All obligations affecting the Premises pursuant to the Administrative Code of the City of New York incurred prior to Closing and payable in money shall be discharged by Seller at or prior to Closing.

11. Seller's Representations. (a) Seller represents and warrants to Purchaser that:

(i) The Premises abut or have a right of access to a public road;

(ii) Seller is the sole owner of the Premises and has the full right, power and authority to sell, convey and transfer the same in accordance with the terms of this contract;

(iii) Seller is not a "foreign person", as that term is defined for purposes of the Foreign Investment in Real Property Tax Act, Internal Revenue Code ("IRC") Section 1445, as amended, and the regulations promulgated thereunder (collectively "FIRPTA");

(iv) The Premises are not affected by any exemptions or abatements of taxes; and

(v) Seller has been known by no other name for the past ten years, except

(b) Seller covenants and warrants that all of the representations and warranties set forth in this contract shall be true and correct at Closing.

(c) Except as otherwise expressly set forth in this contract, none of Seller's covenants, representations, warranties or other obligations contained in this contract shall survive Closing.

12. Condition of Property. Purchaser acknowledges and represents that Purchaser is fully aware of the physical condition and state of repair of the Premises and of all other property included in this sale, based on Purchaser's own inspection and investigation thereof, and that Purchaser is entering into this contract based solely upon such inspection and investigation and not upon any information, data, statements or representations, written or oral, as to the physical condition, state of repair, use, cost of operation or any other matter related to the Premises or the other property included in the sale, given or made by Seller or its representatives, and shall accept the same "as is" in their present condition and state of repair, subject to reasonable use, wear, tear and natural deterioration between the date hereof and the date of Closing (except as otherwise set forth in paragraph 16(f)), without any reduction in the purchase price or claim of any kind for any change in such condition by reason thereof subsequent to the date of this contract. Purchaser and its authorized representatives shall have the right, at reasonable times and upon reasonable notice (by telephone or otherwise) to Seller, to inspect the Premises before Closing.

13. Insurable Title. Seller shall give and Purchaser shall accept such title as

shall be willing to approve and insure in accordance with its standard form of title policy approved by the New York State Insurance Department, subject only to the matters provided for in this contract.

14. Closing, Deed and Title. (a) "Closing" means the settlement of the obligations of Seller and Purchaser to each other under this contract, including the payment of the purchase price to Seller, and the delivery to Purchaser of a

deed in proper statutory short form for record, duly executed and acknowledged, so as to convey to Purchaser fee simple title to the Premises, free of all encumbrances, except as otherwise herein stated. The deed shall contain a covenant by Seller as required by subd. 5 of Section 13 of the Lien Law.

(CONTINUED)

(b) If Seller is a corporation, it shall deliver to Purchaser at the time of Closing (i) a resolution of its Board of Directors authorizing the sale and delivery of the deed, and (ii) a certificate by the Secretary or Assistant Secretary of the corporation certifying such resolution and setting forth facts showing that the transfer is in conformity with the requirements of Section 909 of the Business Corporation Law. The deed in such case shall contain a recital sufficient to establish compliance with that Section.

15. Closing Date and Place. Closing shall take place at the office of

at   o'clock on   19

or, upon reasonable notice (by telephone or otherwise) by Purchaser, at the office of

16. Conditions to Closing. This contract and Purchaser's obligation to purchase the Premises are also subject to and conditioned upon the fulfillment of the following conditions precedent:

(a) The accuracy, as of the date of Closing, of the representations and warranties of Seller made in this contract.

(b) The delivery by Seller to Purchaser of a valid and subsisting Certificate of Occupancy or other required certificate of compliance, or evidence that none was required, covering the building(s) and all of the other improvements located on the property authorizing their use as a   family dwelling at the date of Closing.

(c) The delivery by Seller to Purchaser of a duly executed and sworn affidavit (in form prescribed by law) claiming exemption of the sale contemplated hereby, if such be the case, under Article 31-B of the Tax Law of the State of New York and the Regulations promulgated thereunder, as the same may be amended from time to time (collectively the "Gains Tax Law"); or if such sale shall not be exempt under the Gains Tax Law, Seller and Purchaser agree to comply in a timely manner with the requirements of the Gains Tax Law and, at Closing, Seller shall deliver to Purchaser (i) an official return showing no tax due, or (ii) an official return accompanied by a certified or official bank check drawn on a New York State banking institution payable to the order of the New York State Department of Taxation and Finance in the amount of the tax shown to be due thereon. Seller shall (x) pay promptly any additional tax that may become due under the Gains Tax Law, together with interest and penalties thereon, if any, which may be assessed or become due after Closing, and/or execute any other documents that may be required in respect thereof, and (y) indemnify, defend and save Purchaser harmless from and against any of the foregoing and any damage, liability, cost or expense (including reasonable attorneys' fees) which may be suffered or incurred by Purchaser by reason of the nonpayment thereof. The provisions of this subparagraph (c) shall survive Closing.

(d) The delivery by Seller to Purchaser of a certification stating that Seller is not a foreign person, which certification shall be in the form then required by FIRPTA. If Seller fails to deliver the aforesaid certification or if Purchaser is not entitled under FIRPTA to rely on such certification, Purchaser shall deduct and withhold from the purchase price a sum equal to 10% thereof (or any lesser amount permitted by law) and shall at Closing remit the withheld amount with the required forms to the Internal Revenue Service.

(e) The delivery of the Premises and all building(s) and improvements comprising a part thereof in broom clean condition, vacant and free of leases or tenancies, together with keys to the Premises.

(f) All plumbing (including water supply and septic systems, if any), heating and air conditioning, if any, electrical and mechanical systems, equipment and machinery in the building(s) located on the property and all appliances which are included in this sale being in working order as of the date of Closing.

(g) If the Premises are a one or two family house, delivery by the parties at Closing of affidavits in compliance with state and local law requirements to the effect that there is installed in the Premises a smoke detecting alarm device or devices.

(h) The delivery by the parties of any other affidavits required as a condition of recording the deed.

17. Deed Transfer and Recording Taxes. At Closing, certified or official bank checks payable to the order of the appropriate State, City or County officer in the amount of any applicable transfer and/or recording tax payable by reason of the delivery or recording of the deed or mortgage, if any, shall be delivered by the party required by law or by this contract to pay such transfer and/or recording tax, together with any required tax returns duly executed and sworn to, and such party shall cause any such checks and returns to be delivered to the appropriate officer promptly after Closing. The obligation to pay any additional tax or deficiency and any interest or penalties thereon shall survive Closing.

18. Apportionments and Other Adjustments; Water Meter and Installment Assessments. (a) To the extent applicable, the following shall be apportioned as of midnight of the day before the day of Closing:

(i) taxes, water charges and sewer rents, on the basis of the fiscal period for which assessed; (ii) fuel; (iii) interest on the existing mortgage; (iv) premiums on existing transferable insurance policies and renewals of those expiring prior to Closing; (v) vault charges; (vi) rents as and when collected.

(b) If Closing shall occur before a new tax rate is fixed, the apportionment of taxes shall be upon the basis of the tax rate for the immediately preceding fiscal period applied to the latest assessed valuation.

(c) If there is a water meter on the Premises, Seller shall furnish a reading to a date not more than 30 days before Closing and the unfixed meter charge and sewer rent, if any, shall be apportioned on the basis of such last reading.

(d) If at the date of Closing the Premises are affected by an assessment which is or may become payable in annual installments, and the first installment is then a lien, or has been paid, then for the purposes of this contract all the unpaid installments shall be considered due and shall be paid by Seller at or prior to Closing.

(e) Any errors or omissions in computing apportionments or other adjustments at Closing shall be corrected within a reasonable time following Closing. This subparagraph shall survive Closing.

19. Allowance for Unpaid Taxes, etc. Seller has the option to credit Purchaser as an adjustment to the purchase price with the amount of any unpaid taxes, assessments, water charges and sewer rents, together with any interest and penalties thereon to a date not less than five business days after Closing, provided that official bills therefor computed to said date are produced at Closing.

20. Use of Purchase Price to Remove Encumbrances. If at Closing there are other liens or encumbrances that Seller is obligated to pay or discharge, Seller may use any portion of the cash balance of the purchase price to pay or discharge them, provided Seller shall simultaneously deliver to Purchaser at Closing instruments in recordable form and sufficient to satisfy such liens or encumbrances of record, together with the cost of recording or filing said instruments. As an alternative Seller may deposit sufficient monies with the title insurance company employed by Purchaser acceptable to and required by it to assure their discharge, but only if the title insurance company will insure Purchaser's title clear of the matters or insure against their enforcement out of the Premises and will insure Purchaser's Institutional Lender clear of such matters. Upon notice (by telephone or otherwise), given not less than 3 business days before Closing, Purchaser shall provide separate certified or official bank checks as requested to assist in clearing up these matters.

21. Title Examination; Seller's Inability to Convey; Limitations of Liability. (a) Purchaser shall order an examination of title in respect of the Premises from a title company licensed or authorized to issue title insurance by the New York State Insurance Department or any agent for such title company promptly after the execution of this contract or, if this contract is subject to the mortgage contingency set forth in paragraph 8, after a mortgage commitment has been accepted by Purchaser. Purchaser shall cause a copy of the title report and of any additions thereto to be delivered to the attorney(s) for Seller promptly after receipt thereof.

(b)(i) If at the date of Closing Seller is unable to transfer title to Purchaser in accordance with this contract, or Purchaser has other valid grounds for refusing to close, whether by reason of liens, encumbrances or other objections to title or otherwise (herein collectively called "Defects"), other than those subject to which Purchaser is obligated to accept title hereunder or which Purchaser may have waived and other than those which Seller has herein expressly agreed to remove, remedy or discharge and if Purchaser shall be unwilling to waive the same and to close title without abatement of the purchase price, then, except as hereinafter set forth, Seller shall have the right, at Seller's sole election, either to take such action as Seller may deem advisable to remove, remedy, discharge or comply with such Defects or to cancel this contract; (ii) if Seller elects to take action to remove, remedy or comply with such Defects, Seller shall be entitled from time to time, upon Notice to Purchaser, to adjourn the date for Closing hereunder for a period or periods not exceeding 60 days in the aggregate (but not extending beyond the date upon which Purchaser's mortgage commitment, if any, shall expire), and the date for Closing shall be adjourned to a date specified by Seller not beyond such period. If for any reason whatsoever, Seller shall not have succeeded in removing, remedying or complying with such Defects at the expiration of such adjournment(s), and if Purchaser shall still be unwilling to waive the same and to close title without abatement of the purchase price, then either party may cancel this contract by Notice to the other given within 10 days after such adjourned date; (iii) notwithstanding the foregoing, the existing mortgage (unless this sale is subject to the same) and any matter created by Seller after the date hereof shall be released, discharged or otherwise cured by Seller at or prior to Closing.

(c) If this contract is cancelled pursuant to its terms, other than as a result of Purchaser's default, this contract shall terminate and come to an end, and neither party shall have any further rights, obligations or liabilities against or to the other hereunder or otherwise, except that: (i) Seller shall promptly refund or cause the Escrowee to refund the Downpayment to Purchaser and, unless cancelled as a result of Purchaser's default or pursuant to paragraph 8, to reimburse Purchaser for the net cost of examination of title, including any appropriate additional charges related thereto, and the net cost, if actually paid or incurred by Purchaser, for updating the existing survey of the Premises or of a new survey, and (ii) the obligations under paragraph 27 shall survive the termination of this contract.

22. Affidavit as to Judgments, Bankruptcies, etc. If a title examination discloses judgments, bankruptcies or other returns against persons having names the same as or similar to that of Seller, Seller shall deliver an affidavit at Closing showing that they are not against Seller.

23. Defaults and Remedies. (a) If Purchaser defaults hereunder, Seller's sole remedy shall be to receive and retain the Downpayment as liquidated damages, it being agreed that Seller's damages in case of Purchaser's default might be impossible to ascertain and that the Downpayment constitutes a fair and reasonable amount of damages under the circumstances and is not a penalty.

(CONTINUED)

(b) If Seller defaults hereunder, Purchaser shall have such remedies as Purchaser shall be entitled to at law or in equity, including, but not limited to, specific performance.

24. Purchaser's Lien. All money paid on account of this contract, and the reasonable expenses of examination of title to the Premises and of any survey and survey inspection charges, are hereby made liens on the Premises, but such liens shall not continue after default by Purchaser under this contract.

25. Notices. Any notice or other communication ("Notice") shall be in writing and either (a) sent by either of the parties hereto or by their respective attorneys who are hereby authorized to do so on their behalf or by the Escrowee, by registered or certified mail, postage prepaid, or

(b) delivered in person or by overnight courier, with receipt acknowledged, to the respective addresses given in this contract for the party and the Escrowee, to whom the Notice is to be given, or to such other address as such party or Escrowee shall hereafter designate by Notice given to the other party or parties and the Escrowee pursuant to this paragraph. Each Notice mailed shall be deemed given on the third business day following the date of mailing the same, except that any notice to Escrowee shall be deemed given only upon receipt by Escrowee and each Notice delivered in person or by overnight courier shall be deemed given when delivered.

26. No Assignment. This contract may not be assigned by Purchaser without the prior written consent of Seller in each instance and any purported assignment(s) made without such consent shall be void.

27. Broker. Seller and Purchaser each represents and warrants to the other that it has not dealt with any broker in connection with this sale other than

("Broker") and Seller shall pay Broker any commission earned pursuant to a separate agreement between Seller and Broker. Seller and Purchaser shall indemnify and defend each other against any costs, claims and expenses, including reasonable attorneys' fees, arising out of the breach on their respective parts of any representation or agreement contained in this paragraph. The provisions of this paragraph shall survive Closing or, if Closing does not occur, the termination of this contract.

28. Miscellaneous. (a) All prior understandings, agreements, representations and warranties, oral or written, between Seller and Purchaser are merged in this contract; it completely expresses their full agreement and has been entered into after full investigation, neither party relying upon any statement made by anyone else that is not set forth in this contract.

(b) Neither this contract nor any provision thereof may be waived, changed or cancelled except in writing. This contract shall also apply to and bind the heirs, distributees, legal representatives, successors and permitted assigns of the respective parties. The parties hereby authorize their respective attorneys to agree in writing to any changes in dates and time periods provided for in this contract.

(c) Any singular word or term herein shall also be read as in the plural and the neuter shall include the masculine and feminine gender, whenever the sense of this contract may require it.

(d) The captions in this contract are for convenience of reference only and in no way define, limit or describe the scope of this contract and shall not be considered in the interpretation of this contract or any provision hereof.

(e) This contract shall not be binding or effective until duly executed and delivered by Seller and Purchaser.

(f) Seller and Purchaser shall comply with IRC reporting requirements, if applicable. This subparagraph shall survive Closing.

(g) Each party shall, at any time and from time to time, execute, acknowledge where appropriate and deliver such further instruments and documents and take such other action as may be reasonably requested by the other in order to carry out the intent and purpose of this contract. This subparagraph shall survive Closing.

(h) This contract is intended for the exclusive benefit of the parties hereto and, except as otherwise expressly provided herein, shall not be for the benefit of, and shall not create any rights in, or be enforceable by, any other person or entity.

IN WITNESS WHEREOF, this contract has been duly executed by the parties hereto.

....
Seller   *Purchaser*

....
Seller   *Purchaser*

Attorney for Seller: **Attorney for Purchaser:**

Address: Address:

Tel.:   Fax: Tel.:   Fax:

Receipt of the Downpayment is acknowledged and the undersigned agrees to act in accordance with the provisions of paragraph 6 above.

....
Escrowee

𝕮𝖔𝖓𝖙𝖗𝖆𝖈𝖙 𝖔𝖋 𝕾𝖆𝖑𝖊

TITLE NO.

PREMISES

TO

Section
Block
Lot
County or Town
Street Number Address

FORM 2

A 55—Apartment lease, comprehensive form, rules, guaranty, plain English format. 6-84   PREPARED BY **ARNOLD MANDELL, L.L.B.**   © 1984 BY JULIUS BLUMBERG, INC., PUBLISHER, NYC 10013

LEASE AGREEMENT

The Landlord and Tenant agree to lease the Apartment for the Term and at the Rent stated on these terms:

LANDLORD: **TENANT:**

....

Address for Notices...............................   ....

Apartment (and terrace, if any)..............at
Bank..

Lease date:	Term		Yearly Rent	$
...................19.......	beginning ....19.......		Monthly Rent	$
	ending ....19.......		Security	$
Broker*				

Rider Additional terms on .... page(s) initialed at the end by the parties is attached and made a part of this Lease.

1. Use The Apartment must be used only as a private Apartment to live in as the primary residence of the Tenant and for no other reason. Only a party signing this Lease may use the Apartment. This is subject to Tenant's rights under the Apartment Sharing Law and to limits on the number of people who may legally occupy an Apartment of this size.

2. Failure to give possession Landlord shall not be liable for failure to give Tenant possession of the Apartment on the beginning date of the Term. Rent shall be payable as of the beginning of the Term unless Landlord is unable to give possession. Rent shall then be payable as of the date possession is available. Landlord must give possession within a reasonable time, if not, Tenant may cancel and obtain a refund of money deposited. Landlord will notify Tenant as to the date possession is available. The ending date of the Term will not change.

3. Rent, added rent The rent payment for each month must be paid on the first day of that month at Landlord's address. Landlord need not give notice to pay the rent. Rent must be paid in full without deduction. The first month's rent is to be paid when Tenant signs this Lease. Tenant may be required to pay other charges to Landlord under the terms of this Lease. They are called "added rent." This added rent will be billed and is payable as rent, together with the next monthly rent due. If Tenant fails to pay the added rent on time, Landlord shall have the same rights against Tenant as if Tenant failed to pay rent.

4. Notices Any bill, statement or notice must be in writing. If to Tenant, it must be delivered or mailed to the Tenant at the Apartment. If to Landlord it must be mailed to Landlord's address. It will be considered delivered on the day mailed or if not mailed, when left at the proper address. A notice must be sent by certified mail. Each party must accept and claim the notice given by the other. Landlord must notify Tenant if Landlord's address is changed.

5. Security Tenant has given security to Landlord in the amount stated above. The security has been deposited in the Bank named above and delivery of this Lease is notice of the deposit. If the Bank is not named, Landlord will notify Tenant of the Bank's name and address in which the security is deposited.

If Tenant does not pay rent or added rent on time, Landlord may use the security to pay for rent and added rent then due. If Tenant fails to timely perform any other term in this Lease, Landlord may use the security for payment of money Landlord may spend, or damages Landlord suffers because of Tenant's failure. If the Landlord uses the security Tenant, shall, upon notice from Landlord, send to Landlord an amount equal to the sum used by Landlord. That amount is due, when billed, as rent. At all times Landlord is to have the amount of security stated above.

If Tenant fully performs all terms of this Lease, pays rent on time and leaves the Apartment in good condition on the last day of the Term, then Landlord will return the security being held.

If Landlord sells or leases the Building, Landlord may give the security to the buyer or lessee. In that event Tenant will look only to the buyer or lessee for the return of the security and Landlord will be deemed released. The Landlord may use the security as stated in this section. Landlord may put the security in any place permitted by law. Tenant's security will bear interest only if required by law. Landlord will give Tenant the interest when Landlord is required to return the security to Tenant. Any interest returned to Tenant will be less the sum

Landlord is allowed to keep for expenses. Landlord need not give Tenant interest on the security if Tenant is in default.

6. Services Landlord will supply: (a) heat as required by law, (b) hot and cold water for bathroom and kitchen sink, (c) use of elevator, if any, and (d) cooling if central air conditioning is installed. Landlord is not required to install air-conditioning. Stopping or reducing of service(s) will not be reason for Tenant to stop paying rent, to make a money claim or to claim eviction. Tenant may enforce its rights under the warranty of habitability. Damage to the equipment or appliances supplied by Landlord, caused by Tenant's act or neglect, may be repaired by Landlord at Tenant's expense. The repair cost will be added rent.

Tenant must pay for all electric, gas, telephone and other utility services used in the Apartment and arrange for them with the public utility company. Tenant must not use a dishwasher, washing machine, dryer, freezer, heater, ventilator, air cooling equipment or other appliance unless installed by Landlord or with Landlord's written consent. Tenant must not use more electric than the wiring or feeders to the Building can safely carry.

Landlord may stop service of the plumbing, heating, elevator, air cooling or electrical systems, because of accident, emergency, repairs, or changes until the work is complete.

If Landlord wants to change a person operated elevator to an automatic elevator, Landlord may stop service on 10 days' notice. Landlord will then have a reasonable time to begin installation of an automatic type elevator.

7. Alteration Tenant must obtain Landlord's prior written consent to install any panelling, flooring, "built in" decorations, partitions, railings, or make alterations or to paint or wallpaper the Apartment. Tenant must not change the plumbing, ventilating, air conditioning, electric or heating systems. If consent is given, the alterations and installations shall become the property of Landlord when completed and paid for. They shall remain with and as part of the Apartment at the end of the Term. Landlord has the right to demand that Tenant remove the alterations and installations before the end of the Term. The demand shall be by notice, given at least 15 days before the end of the Term. Tenant shall comply with the demand at Tenant's own cost. Landlord is not required to do or pay for any work unless stated in this Lease.

If a lien is filed on the Apartment or Building for any reason relating to Tenant's fault, Tenant must immediately pay or bond the amount stated in the Lien. Landlord may pay or bond the lien if Tenant fails to do so within 20 days after Tenant has notice about the Lien. Landlord's costs shall be added rent.

8. Repairs Tenant must take good care of the Apartment and all equipment and fixtures in it. Landlord will repair the plumbing, heating and electrical systems. Tenant must, at Tenant's cost, make all repairs and replacements whenever the need results from Tenant's act or neglect. If Tenant fails to make a needed repair or replacement, Landlord may do it. Landlord's reasonable expense will be added rent.

9. Fire, accident, defects, damage Tenant must give Landlord prompt notice of fire, accident, damage or dangerous or defective condition. If the Apartment can not be used because of fire or other casualty, Tenant is not required to pay rent for the time the Apartment is unusable. If part of the Apartment can not be used, Tenant must pay rent for the usable part. Landlord shall have the right to decide which part of the Apartment is usable. Landlord need only repair the damaged

(CONTINUED)

part of the Apartment. Landlord is not required to repair or replace any fixtures, furnishings or decorations but only equipment that is originally installed by Landlord. Landlord is not responsible for delays due to settling insurance claims, obtaining estimates, labor and supply problems or any other cause not fully under Landlord's control.

If the apartment can not be used, Landlord has 30 days to decide whether to repair it. Landlord's decision to repair must be given by notice to Tenant within 30 days of the fire or casualty. Landlord shall have a reasonable time to repair. In determining what is a reasonable time, consideration shall be given to any delays in receipt of insurance settlements, labor trouble and causes not within Landlord's control. If Landlord fails to give Tenant notice of its decision within 30 days, Tenant may cancel the lease as of the date of the fire or casualty. The cancellation shall be effective only if it is given before Landlord begins to repair or before Landlord notifies Tenant of its decision to repair. If the fire or other casualty is caused by an act or neglect of Tenant or guest of Tenant all repairs will be made at Tenant's expense and Tenant must pay the full rent with no adjustment. The cost of the repairs will be added rent.

Landlord has the right to demolish, rebuild or renovate the Building if there is substantial damage by fire or other casualty. Even if the Apartment is not damaged, Landlord may cancel this Lease within 30 days after the substantial fire or casualty by giving Tenant notice of Landlord's intention to demolish, rebuild or renovate. The Lease will end 30 days after Landlord's cancellation notice to Tenant. Tenant must deliver the Apartment to Landlord on or before the cancellation date in the notice and pay all rent due to the date of the fire or casualty. If the Lease is cancelled Landlord is not required to repair the Apartment or Building. The cancellation does not release Tenant of liability in connection with the fire or casualty. This Section is intended to replace the terms of New York Real Property Law Section 227.

10. Liability   Landlord is not liable for loss, expense, or damage to any person or property, unless due to Landlord's negligence. Landlord is not liable to Tenant for permitting or refusing entry of anyone into the Building.

Tenant must pay for damages suffered and reasonable expenses of Landlord relating to any claim arising from any act or neglect of Tenant. If an action is brought against Landlord arising from Tenant's act or neglect Tenant shall defend Landlord at Tenant's expense with an attorney of Landlord's choice.

Tenant is responsible for all acts or neglect of Tenant's family, employees, guests or invitees.

11. Entry by Landlord   Landlord may enter the Apartment at reasonable hours to: repair, inspect, exterminate, install or work on master antennas or other systems or equipment and perform other work that Landlord decides is necessary or desirable. At reasonable hours Landlord may show the Apartment to possible buyers, lenders, or tenants of the entire Building or land. At reasonable hours Landlord may show the Apartment to possible or new tenants during the last 4 months of the Term. Entry by Landlord must be on reasonable notice except in emergency.

12. Assignment and sublease   Tenant must not assign all or part of this Lease or sublet all or part of the Apartment or permit any other person to use the Apartment. If Tenant does, Landlord has the right to cancel the Lease as stated in the Tenant's Default section. State law may permit Tenant to sublet under certain conditions. Tenant must get Landlord's written permission each time Tenant wants to assign or sublet. Permission to assign or sublet is good only for that assignment or sublease. Tenant remains bound to the terms of this lease after a assignment or sublet is permitted, even if Landlord accepts money from the assignee or subtenant. The amount accepted will be credited toward money due from Tenant, as Landlord shall determine. The assignee or subtenant does not become Landlord's tenant. Tenant is responsible for acts and neglect of any person in the Apartment.

13. Subordination   This Lease and Tenant's rights, are subject and subordinate to all present and future: (a) leases for the Building or the land on which it stands, (b) mortgages on the leases or the Building or land, (c) agreements securing money paid or to be paid by a lender, and (d) terms, conditions, renewals, changes of any kind and extensions of the mortgages, leases or lender agreements. Tenant must promptly execute any certificate(s) that Landlord requests to show that this Lease is so subject and subordinate. Tenant authorizes Landlord to sign these certificate(s) for Tenant.

14. Condemnation   If all of the Apartment or Building is taken or condemned by a legal authority, the Term, and Tenant's rights shall end as of the date the authority takes title to the Apartment or Building. If any part of the Apartment or Building is taken, Landlord may cancel this Lease on notice to Tenant. The notice shall set a cancellation date not less than 30 days from the date of the notice. If the Lease is cancelled, Tenant must deliver the Apartment to Landlord on the cancellation date together with all rent due to that date. The entire award for any taking belongs to Landlord. Tenant assigns to Landlord any interest Tenant may have to any part of the award. Tenant shall make no claim for the value of the remaining part of the Term.

15. Construction or demolition   Construction or demolition may be performed in or near the Building. Even if it interferes with Tenant's ventilation, view or enjoyment of the Apartment it shall not affect Tenant's obligations in this Lease.

16. Tearing down the building   If the Landlord wants to tear down the entire Building, Landlord shall have the right to end this Lease by giving six (6) months notice to Tenant. If Landlord gives Tenant such notice and such notice was given to every residential tenant in the Building, then the Lease will end and Tenant must leave the Apartment at the end of the 6 month period in the notice.

17. Liability for property left with Landlord's employees   Landlord's employees are not permitted to drive Tenant's cars or care for Tenant's cars or personal property. Tenant must not leave a car or other personal property with any of Landlord's employees. Landlord is not responsible for (a) loss, theft or damage to the property, and (b) injury caused by the property or its use.

18. Playground, pool, parking and recreation areas   If there is a playground, pool, parking or recreation area, Landlord may give Tenant permission to use it. Tenant will use the area at Tenant's own risk and must pay all fees Landlord charges. Landlord's permission may be cancelled at any time.

19. Terraces and balconies   The Apartment may have a terrace or balcony. The terms of this Lease apply to the terrace or balcony as if part of the Apartment. The Landlord may make special rules for the terrace and balcony. Landlord will notify Tenant of such rules.

Tenant must keep the terrace or balcony clean and free from snow, ice, leaves and garbage and keep all screens and drains in good repair. No cooking is allowed on the terrace or balcony. Tenant may not keep plants, or install a fence or any addition on the terrace or balcony. If Tenant does, Landlord has the right to remove and store them at Tenant's expense.

Tenant is responsible to make all repairs to the terrace or balcony at its sole expense regardless of the cause and whether or not existing prior to Tenant's occupancy. Tenant shall maintain the terrace and balcony in good repair.

20. Tenant's certificate   Upon request by Landlord, Tenant shall sign a certificate stating the following: (1) This Lease is in full force and unchanged (or if changed, how it was changed); and (2) Landlord has fully performed all of the terms of this Lease and Tenant has no claim against Landlord; and (3) Tenant is fully performing all the terms of the Lease and will continue to do so; (4) rent and added rent have been paid to date; and (5) any other reasonable statement required by Landlord. The certificate will be addressed to the party Landlord chooses.

21. Correcting Tenant's defaults   If Tenant fails to timely correct a default after notice from Landlord, Landlord may correct it at Tenant's expense. Landlord's costs to correct the default shall be added rent.

22. Tenant's duty to obey laws and regulations   Tenant must, at Tenant's expense, promptly comply with all laws, orders, rules, requests, and directions, of all governmental authorities, Landlord's insurers, Board of Fire Underwriters, or similar groups. Notices received by Tenant from any authority or group must be promptly delivered to Landlord. Tenant may not do anything which may increase Landlord's insurance premiums. If Tenant does, Tenant must pay the increase in premium as added rent.

23. Tenant's default   A. Landlord must give Tenant written notice of default stating the type of default. The following are defaults and must be cured by Tenant within the time stated:
(1) Failure to pay rent or added rent on time, 3 days.

226

(CONTINUED)

(2) Failure to move into the Apartment within 15 days after the beginning date of the Term, 10 days.

(3) Issuance of a court order under which the Apartment may be taken by another party, 10 days.

(4) Improper conduct by Tenant annoying other tenants, 10 days.

(5) Failure to comply with any other term or Rule in the Lease, 10 days.

If Tenant fails to cure the default in the time stated, Landlord may cancel the Lease by giving Tenant a cancellation notice. The cancellation notice will state the date the Term will end which may be no less than 10 days after the date of the notice. On the cancellation date in the notice the Term of this Lease shall end. Tenant must leave the Apartment and give Landlord the keys on or before the cancellation date. Tenant continues to be responsible as stated in this Lease. If the default can not be cured in the time stated, Tenant must begin to cure within that time and continue diligently until cured.

B. If Tenant's application for the Apartment contains any material misstatement of fact, Landlord may cancel this Lease. Cancellation shall be by cancellation notice as stated in Section 23.A.

C. If (1) the Lease is cancelled; or (2) rent or added rent is not paid on time; or (3) Tenant vacates the Apartment, Landlord may, in addition to other remedies, take any of the following steps: (a) peacefully enter the Apartment and remove Tenant and any person or property, and (b) use eviction or other lawsuit method to take back the Apartment.

D. If this Lease is cancelled, or Landlord takes back the Apartment, the following takes place:

(1) Rent and added rent for the unexpired Term becomes due and payable.

(2) Landlord may relet the Apartment and anything in it. The reletting may be for any term. Landlord may charge any rent or no rent and give allowances to the new tenant. Landlord may, at Tenant's expense, do any work Landlord reasonably feels needed to put the Apartment in good repair and prepare it for renting. Tenant stays liable and is not released except as provided by law.

(3) Any rent received by Landlord for the re-renting shall be used first to pay Landlord's expenses and second to pay any amounts Tenant owes under this Lease. Landlord's expenses include the costs of getting possession and re-renting the Apartment, including, but not only reasonable legal fees, brokers fees, cleaning and repairing costs, decorating costs and advertising costs.

(4) From time to time Landlord may bring actions for damages. Delay or failure to bring an action shall not be a waiver of Landlord's rights. Tenant is not entitled to any excess of rents collected over the rent paid by Tenant to Landlord under this Lease.

(5) If Landlord relets the Apartment combined with other space an adjustment will be made based on square footage. Money received by Landlord from the next tenant other than the monthly rent, shall not be considered as part of the rent paid to Landlord. Landlord is entitled to all of it.

If Landlord relets the Apartment the fact that all or part of the next tenant's rent is not collected does not affect Tenant's liability. Landlord has no duty to collect the next tenant's rent. Tenant must continue to pay rent, damages, losses and expenses without offset.

E. If Landlord takes possession of the Apartment by Court order, or under the Lease, Tenant has no right to return to the Apartment.

24. Jury trial and counterclaims Landlord and Tenant agree not to use their right to a Trial by Jury in any action or proceeding brought by either, against the other, for any matter concerning this Lease or the Apartment. This does not include actions for personal injury or property damage. Tenant gives up any right to bring a counterclaim or set-off in any action or proceeding by Landlord against Tenant on any matter directly or indirectly related to this Lease or Apartment.

25. No waiver, illegality Landlord's acceptance of rent or failure to enforce any term in this Lease is not a waiver of any of Landlord's rights. If a term in this Lease is illegal, the rest of this lease remains in full force.

26. Insolvency If (1) Tenant assigns property for the benefit of creditors, or (2) a non-bankruptcy trustee or receiver of Tenant or Tenant's property is appointed, Landlord may give Tenant 30 days notice of cancellation of the Term of this Lease. If any of the above is not fully dismissed within the 30 days, the

Term shall end as of the date stated in the notice. Tenant must continue to pay rent, damages, losses and expenses without offset. If Tenant files a voluntary petition in bankruptcy or an involuntary petition in bankruptcy is filed against Tenant, Landlord may not terminate this Lease.

27. Rules Tenant must comply with these Rules. Notice of new Rules will be given to Tenant. Landlord need not enforce Rules against other Tenants. Landlord is not liable to Tenant if another tenant violates these Rules. Tenant receives no rights under these Rules:

(1) The comfort or rights of other Tenants must not be interfered with. This means that annoying sounds, smells and lights are not allowed.

(2) No one is allowed on the roof. Nothing may be placed on or attached to fire escapes, sills, windows or exterior walls of the Apartment or in the hallways or public areas.

(3) Tenant may not operate manual elevators. Smoking is not permitted in elevators. Messengers and trade people must use service elevators and service entrances. Bicycles are not allowed on passenger elevators.

(4) Tenant must give to Landlord keys to all locks. Doors must be locked at all times. Windows must be locked when Tenant is out.

(5) Apartment floors must be covered by carpets or rugs. No waterbeds allowed in Apartments.

(6) Dogs, cats or other animals or pets are not allowed in the Apartment or Building.

(7) Garbage disposal rules must be followed. Wash lines, vents and plumbing fixtures must be used for their intended purpose.

(8) Laundry machines, if any, are used at Tenant's risk and cost. Instructions must be followed.

(9) Moving furniture, fixtures or equipment must be scheduled with Landlord. Tenant must not send Landlord's employees on personal errands.

(10) Improperly parked cars may be removed without notice at Tenant's cost.

(11) Tenant must not allow the cleaning of the windows or other part of the Apartment or Building from the outside.

(12) Tenant shall conserve energy.

28. Representations, changes in Lease Tenant has read this Lease. All promises made by the Landlord are in this Lease. There are no others. This Lease may be changed only by an agreement in writing signed by and delivered to each party.

29. Landlord unable to perform If due to labor trouble, government order, lack of supply, Tenant's act or neglect, or any other cause not fully within Landlord's reasonable control, Landlord is delayed or unable to (a) carry out any of Landlord's promises or agreements, (b) supply any service required to be supplied, (c) make any required repair or change in the Apartment or Building, or (d) supply any equipment or appliances Landlord is required to supply, this Lease shall not be ended or Tenant's obligations affected.

30. End of term At the end of the Term, Tenant must: leave the Apartment clean and in good condition, subject to ordinary wear and tear; remove all of Tenant's property and all Tenant's installations and decorations; repair all damages to the Apartment and Building caused by moving; and restore the Apartment to its condition at the beginning of the Term. If the last day of the Term is on a Saturday, Sunday or State or Federal holiday the Term shall end on the prior business day.

31. Space "as is" Tenant has inspected the Apartment and Building. Tenant states they are in good order and repair and takes the Apartment as is except for latent defects.

32. Landlord's warranty of habitability Landlord states that the Apartment and Building are fit for human living and there is no condition dangerous to health, life or safety.

33. Landlord's consent If Tenant requires Landlord's consent to any act and such consent is not given, Tenant's only right is to ask the Court for a declaritory judgment to force Landlord to give consent. Tenant agrees not to make any claim against Landlord for money or subtract any sum from the rent because such consent was not given.

34. Limit of recovery against Landlord Tenant is limited to Landlord's interest in the Building for payment of a judgment or other court remedy against Landlord.

(CONTINUED)

35. Lease binding on This Lease is binding on Landlord and Tenant and their heirs, distributees, executors, administrators, successors and lawful assigns.

36. Landlord Landlord means the owner (Building or Apartment), or the lessee of the Building, or a lender in possession. Landlord's obligations end when Landlord's interest in the (Building or Apartment) is transferred. Any acts Landlord may do may be performed by Landlord's agents or employees.

37. Paragraph headings The paragraph headings are for convenience only.

38. Furnishings If the Apartment is furnished, the furniture and other furnishings are accepted as is. If an inventory is supplied each party shall have a signed copy. At the end of the Term Tenant shall return the furniture and other furnishings clean and in good order and repair. Tenant is not responsible for ordinary wear and damage by the elements.

39. Broker If the name of a Broker appears in the box at the top of the first page of this Lease, Tenant states that this is the only Broker that showed the Apartment to Tenant. If a Broker's name does not appear Tenant states that no agent or broker showed Tenant the Apartment. Tenant will pay Landlord any money Landlord may spend if either statement is incorrect.

Signatures, effective date Landlord and Tenant have signed this Lease as of the above date. It is effective when Landlord delivers to Tenant a copy signed by all parties.

LANDLORD: TENANT:

....

WITNESS:..   ....

GUARANTY OF PAYMENT

Guarantor and address   Date of Guaranty   ....19........

....

1. Reason for guaranty I know that the Landlord would not rent the Apartment to the Tenant unless I guarantee Tenant's performance. I have also requested the Landlord to enter into the Lease with the Tenant. I have a substantial interest in making sure that the Landlord rents the Premises to the Tenant.

2. Guaranty I guaranty the full performance of the Lease by the Tenant. This Guaranty is absolute and without any condition. It includes, but is not limited to, the payment of rent and other money charges.

3. Changes in Lease have no effect This Guaranty will not be affected by any change in the Lease, whatsoever. This includes, but is not limited to, any extension of time or renewals. The Guaranty will bind me even if I am not a party to these changes.

4. Waiver of Notice I do not have to be informed about any default by Tenant. I waive notice of nonpayment or other default.

5. Performance If the Tenant defaults, the Landlord may require me to perform without first demanding that the Tenant perform.

6. Waiver of jury trial I give up my right to trial by jury in any claim related to the Lease or this Guaranty.

7. Changes This Guaranty can be changed only by written agreement signed by all parties to the Lease and this Guaranty.

Signatures   GUARANTOR:...

WITNESS:..   Guarantor's address:...

STATE OF	, COUNTY OF	ss.:	STATE OF	, COUNTY OF	ss.:

STATE OF   , COUNTY OF   ss.:   STATE OF   , COUNTY OF   ss.:

On   19   , before me personally   On   19   , before me personally

came   to me known, who,   came

being by me duly sworn, did depose and say that deponent resides at No.

deponent is   of

the corporation described in and which executed, the foregoing instrument; deponent knows the seal of said corporation; that the seal affixed to said instrument is such corporate seal; that it was so affixed by order of the Board of Directors of said corporation; deponent signed deponent's name thereto by like order.

to me known to be the individual   described in, and who executed the foregoing instrument, and acknowledged that   he   executed the same.

FORM 3

𝔇𝔢𝔢𝔡

This Deed is made on August 25, 1997
BETWEEN
Sally Seller

whose post office address is
123 Main Street
Fair Lawn N.J. 07410
referred to as the Grantor,
AND
Bill Buyer

whose post office address is
321 Boulevard
Rockville Centre, N.Y. 11570
referred to as the Grantee.
The words "Grantor" and "Grantee" shall mean all Grantors and all Grantees listed above.

1. Transfer of Ownership. The Grantor grants and conveys (transfers ownership of) the property (called the "Property") described below to the Grantee. This transfer is made for the sum of
$150,000
The Grantor acknowledges receipt of this money.

2. Tax Map Reference. (N.J.S.A. 46:15-1.1) Municipality of Fair Lawn
Block No. 4407   Lot No. 234   Account No.
☐ No property tax identification number is available on the date of this Deed. (Check box if applicable.)

3. Property. The Property consists of the land and all the buildings and structures on the land in
the Borough   of Fair Lawn
County of Bergen   and State of New Jersey. The legal description is:

☒ Please see attached Legal Description annexed hereto and made a part hereof (check box if applicable).

Prepared by: (print signer's name below signature)	(For Recorder's Use Only)
_____	

229

(CONTINUED)

The street address of the Property is:
123 Main Street, Fair Lawn N.J. 07410

4. Promises by Grantor. The Grantor promises that the Grantor has done no act to encumber the Property. This promise is called a "covenant as to grantor's acts" (N.J.S.A. 46:4-6). This promise means that the Grantor has not allowed anyone else to obtain any legal rights which affect the Property (such as by making a mortgage or allowing a judgment to be entered against the Grantor).

5. Signatures. The Grantor signs this Deed as of the date at the top of the first page. (Print name below each signature).

Witnessed By:

_____(Seal)
Saller Seller, single

_____   _____(Seal)

STATE OF New Jersey   , COUNTY OF Bergen
I CERTIFY that on August 25, 1997
Salle Seller, single,

personally came before me and stated to my satisfaction that this person (or if more than one, each person):
(a) was the maker of this Deed;
(b) executed this Deed as his or her own act; and,

(c) made this Deed for $ 150,000.00   as the full and actual consideration paid or to be paid for the transfer of title. (Such consideration is defined in N.J.S.A. 46:15-5.)

RECORD AND RETURN TO:	
Ganz & Sivin, P.A.	
Attn. David L. Ganz, Esq.	_____
5 Ryder Road (Box 1215)	(Print name and title below signature)
Fair Lawn N.J. 07410	David L. Ganz
	Attorney at Law State of New Jersey

103 - Deed - Bargain and Sale
Cov. to Grantor's Act - Ind. to Ind. or Corp.
Plain Language 9511-1

Index